OUR MARYLAND

First edition printed April 1987
© 1987 Gibbs M. Smith, Inc.

93 92 91 90 89   5 4 3

Design by J. Scott Knudsen
Interior production by Smith & Clarkson

Cover photos:

Victor B. Giordano—crabs, Baltimore, park
policeman, clarinetist

Maryland Office of Tourism—barns, children
on dock

Library of Congress Cataloging-in-Publication Data
Eagen, Jane 1930-
    Our Maryland

    Includes index.
    Summary: Explores the social, political, economic, and
cultural history and geography of Maryland from prehistory
to the present.
    1. Maryland—Juvenile literature. [1. Maryland]
I. McGinnes. Jeanne, 1923–   II. Title.
F181.3.E24   1987   975.2   86-30380
ISBN 0-87905-233-3

OUR MARYLAND

Jane Eagen
Jeanne McGinnis

➜
GIBBS M. SMITH, INC.
Peregrine Smith Books
Salt Lake City
1987

Table of Contents

Table of Maps and Charts

Artists' prints like this one show us what Maryland was like in the early days. This is a view of Point Lookout. If a photograph were taken from an airplane today, how might a view of Maryland be different from an artist's drawing in the 1800s?

Foreword

You ou probably know that the Pilgrims came to Plymouth Rock on a ship called the *Mayflower*. But did you know that the Maryland settlers came on two ships called the *Ark* and the *Dove?*

You may have heard of a document the Pilgrims wrote called the Mayflower Compact. But did you know that Maryland's settlement was based on a charter which gave them some of the most important freedoms we still enjoy as Americans?

You probably studied the famous Boston Tea Party. Remember that the Boston patriots dressed up as Indians and threw boxes of tea into the harbor. But did you know that Maryland had two exciting tea parties? One was in Chestertown, and one was in Annapolis. And in Annapolis, the ship was actually set on fire!

We all know that George Washington was America's first president. But is that true? He was our first president under the United States Constitution. But a Maryland man named John Hanson was America's first president under the Articles of Confederation. That set of rules governed America before our federal Constitution was approved.

There are so many exciting events and interesting people in Maryland's past. You can take part in the events and meet the people, right in the pages of this book.

I still love to read about Maryland history, even though I've been out of school for many years. I hope this book will also help you develop a lifelong interest in our great state. It has a wonderful heritage and has made many contributions to the history of our great country.

Louis L. Goldstein
Comptroller of Maryland, 1958 to the present

Loy's Station Bridge in Thurmont. Many towns in our state have remains from the past, such as this bridge.

Introduction

Cumberland • Frostburg • Hagerstown • Frederick • Baltimore • Annapolis • Columbia • Bowie • Westminster • Havre de Grace • Salisbury • Ocean City • Chestertown • Crisfield • Elkton • Oakland • Hancock • Rockville • Waldorf • Lexington Park • Solomons • Centerville • Denton • Cambridge • Rock Hall • Easton • Towson • St. Michael's • St. Mary's City • St. Clement's Island.

How many of these names do you recognize? Can you find them on a map of Maryland? Do you know in which counties they can be found? Do you know why these places are important in the history of Maryland?

The Old Line State • The Free State • America in Miniature. These are all nicknames for Maryland. Each one gives a clue to the distinct *character* of our state.

The state's land and water forms and the climate have helped decide the way Marylanders live. The people and their ideals have made Maryland what it is today. Over the years, part of the state has changed to a chain of growing cities. Nearly half of the state remains forest land.

In this book, we will study the people and land of the past. We will learn about changes over the years. We will see how the Maryland of today took shape.

MARYLAND IN THE UNITED STATES

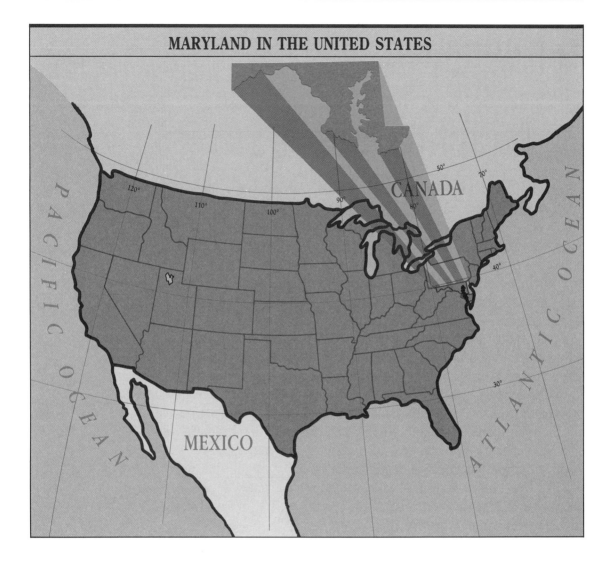

Maryland's Geography

1

Boundaries

In the universe, in the Milky Way Galaxy, in the solar system, on the planet earth, in the western and northern hemispheres, on the continent of North America, in the United States lies the state of Maryland. This address in the universe is a key to understanding how people have lived in Maryland for thousands of years.

The area of Maryland is 12,186 square miles. Of this, 9,837 square miles is land, and 2,349 square miles is water. There are only eight states in the United States that are smaller than Maryland.

Maryland has two outstanding features. The first is its unusual shape. The second is the large body of water inside Maryland's *boundary*.

Maryland is bordered by four states. Look at them on the map of Maryland, page 12. Name the four states that touch Maryland. What else borders our state on the east?

The map of Maryland shows two different kinds of boundary lines. Some are straight lines, and some are crooked, wiggly lines. The straight lines were *surveyed* (marked off) and agreed upon by people. The crooked line follows a *natural* feature—the Potomac River.

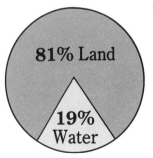

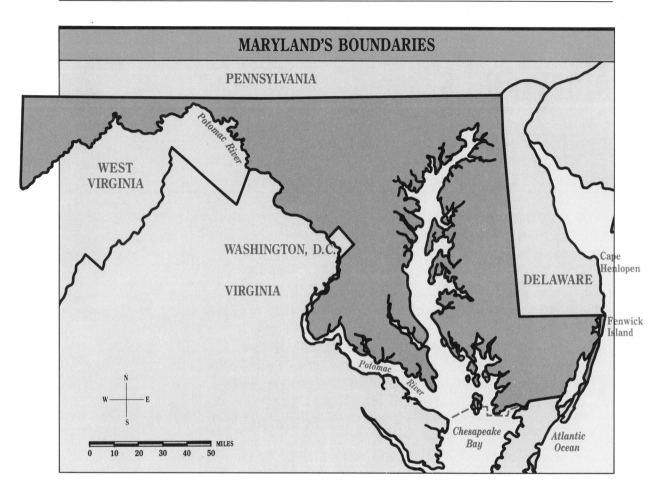

MARYLAND'S BOUNDARIES

Boundary Disputes

The boundaries of Maryland were first set by Charles I (Charles the first), king of England, when he gave the land to Lord Baltimore. These lines have changed several times. They were argued over for many years before they were finally settled.

Maps drawn in the 1600s (when white people first came here) were not always correct. This caused many problems later on. For one, Cape Henlopen on the Atlantic coast was to be the starting point of the line which separated Maryland and Delaware. A map maker placed this line twenty miles off course on the map the king used. The result is that the

Maryland-Delaware line begins at Fenwick Island instead of Cape Henlopen.

Many maps and land surveys, though, were almost perfect. In 1763 Charles Mason and Jeremiah Dixon were hired as *surveyors*. Their task was to mark the boundary between Maryland, Pennsylvania, and Delaware. They marked each mile with a pile of stones. Every fifth mile got a special marker. On the side of the stone facing Maryland was a mark that stood for Lord Baltimore, the state's *founder*. On the other side was a mark that stood for William Penn, the founder of Pennsylvania. This survey proved to be very accurate when it was checked using more modern tools years later. Today it is still known as the Mason-Dixon line.

Maryland's western boundary was to have been the south bank of the most western branch of the Potomac River. This area, which is now West Virginia, had not been fully explored when the agreement was reached with Virginia. The northern branch of the Potomac River was used. Later it was found that the southern branch was farther west. Both Maryland and Virginia claimed the land between the two branches. It was decided in a court of law that this land should go to Virginia. The reason was that the people of Virginia had settled the land.

Mason-Dixon marker.

The part of the southern boundary in the Chesapeake Bay was another problem. Once again, *inaccurate* maps caused trouble. The value of oysters in 1870 made this area very important to both Maryland and Virginia. Finally, a third party decided where the border should be. A jagged line was decided upon. It was accepted by both states.

Chesapeake Bay Estuary

The Susquehanna River used to be where the Chesapeake Bay is today. The river and its many *tributaries* (branches) ran through Maryland into Virginia. Little by little, much of the land on both sides of the river sank. Ocean water flowed into

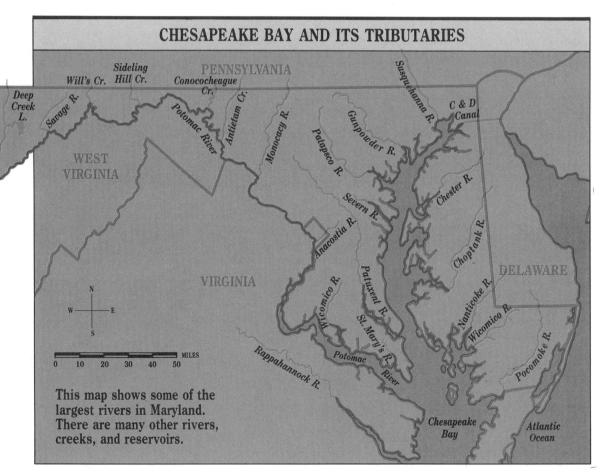

CHESAPEAKE BAY AND ITS TRIBUTARIES

This map shows some of the largest rivers in Maryland. There are many other rivers, creeks, and reservoirs.

View of Calvert Cliffs.

part of the Susquehanna River and its tributaries. This formed the Chesapeake Bay.

The Chesapeake Bay is an *estuary* (ES-tyew-air-ee). An estuary is the part of the river system that is drowned.

The shore line of the Chesapeake Bay is very *irregular*. This makes many harbors and coves that are safe places for boats to dock. Although the Chesapeake Bay is less than 200 miles long, its coast line is 3,600 miles long. That's long enough to reach from the Atlantic Ocean to Hawaii!

One interesting part of the bay coast line is Calvert Cliffs. The cliffs rise up to 100 feet above the water. Different layers of rock, *fossils,* and soil can be seen. (Fossils are hardened remains of plants and animals.) Geologists study the cliffs to learn more about how the Chesapeake Bay was formed. Fossils of animals that lived here millions of years ago can be found on the shore.

Ecosystem

The Chesapeake Bay is an *ecosystem*. This means that the weather, air, land, water, plants, and animals all act together in a community. Each affects the others.

Many small animals feed on the plant life. Larger animals, called *carnivores,* eat the smaller ones. People, called *omnivores,* are at the top of the chain. They eat both plants and animals. From the Chesapeake Bay, we eat many different kinds of shellfish and finfish.

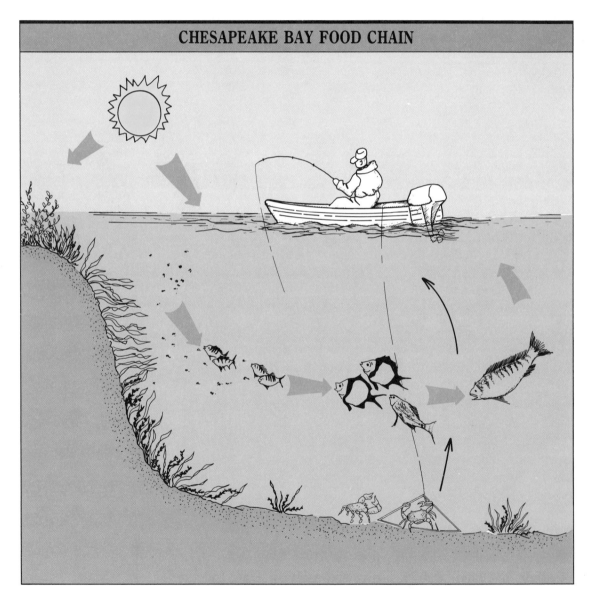

CHESAPEAKE BAY FOOD CHAIN

Keeping this food chain working has become harder. Rain and wind *erode* (wear away) the soil in the *drainage basin* of the Chesapeake Bay. This causes the water to become muddy, and less sunlight reaches the plants. The first link of the food chain is made weak. *Pollution* further spoils the water. Fertilizer from farms washes into the rivers. Waste from factories also causes trouble for living things. Oil spills and other waste products from the thousands of ships in the bay are very harmful to the plants and animals that live there. Fallout from dirty air adds to the problem of keeping the Chesapeake Bay ecosystem healthy.

This striped bass has been tagged at the Joseph Manning Fish Hatchery. If caught by a fisherman, some details about the fish's travels can be recorded by the Department of Natural Resources. The striped bass migrates from brackish to fresh water.

Salt in the Bay

The *salinity,* or amount of salt in the water, changes from place to place. It also changes with the season of the year. The ocean brings in salt water. It mixes with the fresh water from the rivers and creeks.

There is less salt in the northern part of the Chesapeake Bay than in the southern part. There are two reasons for this.

Crabs from the Chesapeake Bay.

First, the rivers are pouring in fresh water. Second, the *tidal current* from the ocean gets weaker the further it stretches. The salinity is much greater in the Potomac River than in the Patapsco River. It is greater in the eastern part of the bay than in the western part. The mouth of the Choptank River is saltier than the mouth of the Patuxent River. Salinity is greater in autumn than in spring. In spring the rivers carry more water from rain and melting snow.

Brackish water is a mix of fresh and salt water. Many sea animals move from brackish to fresh or salt water during the year. Some fish need fresh water for laying eggs. Salinity also affects the flavor of shellfish. The water being different from place to place in the Chesapeake Bay allows hundreds of different things to live there.

Marshes

There are 212,000 acres of marsh, or wetland. Marshes are sometimes called protein factories. Here live the many plants and small animals needed to feed the larger animals. Land developers sometimes drain marshes to build new homes and businesses. This upsets the whole ecosystem. For this reason, laws have been made to protect the valuable wetlands of Maryland. Controlling the use of the marshes is hard.

Tides

The difference between high tide and low tide in the
Chesapeake Bay is less than three feet. It is between one and
two feet in most of Maryland. The tide changes twice every
24 to 25 hours. The Chesapeake Bay is such a large estuary
that the tides also enter the mouths of the rivers. This part of
Maryland is called Tidewater Maryland.

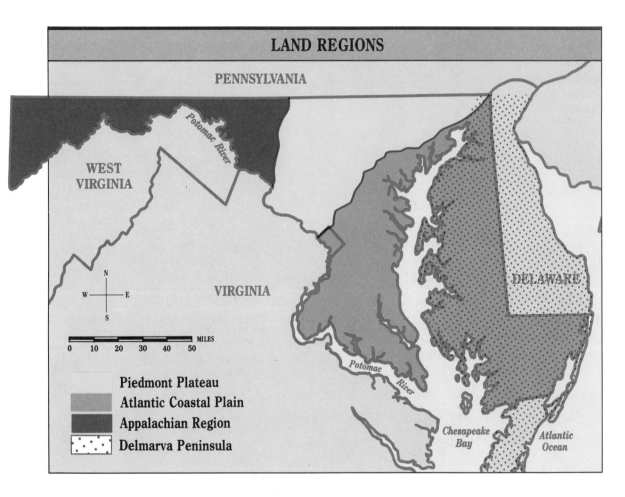

Atlantic Coastal Plain

The land along the Chesapeake Bay and the Atlantic Ocean is
part of the Atlantic Coastal Plain. It is lowland with few hills.

Its *elevation* (height above sea level) is less than 100 feet. The land is light and sandy and is good for farming. There are few rocks or boulders. There are many rivers and creeks. No part of the Atlantic Coastal Plain in Maryland is very far from water. Because water cools and heats more slowly than land, this helps even out the temperature in the Atlantic Coastal Plain. The temperatures here are more mild than in the rest of Maryland.

Can you tell what crop is growing on this large farm in the Atlantic Coastal Plain?

This machinery is making the Chesapeake and Delaware Canal deeper by digging out tons of mud.

The land east of the Chesapeake Bay is called the Delmarva *Peninsula*. It contains all of Delaware and parts of Maryland and Virginia. Its name uses letters from each of these three states:

DEL – Delaware

MAR – Maryland

VA – Virginia.

The Chesapeake and Delaware Canal in the Coastal Plain is not a natural waterway. It was built in 1829 to shorten the distance between Baltimore and the Atlantic Ocean.

Today the eastern shore and western shore are connected by the Chesapeake Bay Bridge.

The Piedmont Plateau

Most rivers in Maryland can be *navigated* up to the point where there are waterfalls. Many can also be navigated on the other side of the falls. If you placed an *X* on the falls of each river and then connected the *X*s, you would draw the *fall line*. It is here that the hilly Piedmont Plateau (pla-TOH) begins. (A plateau is a high, flat area.) Large rocks are found in some places. The plateau is between 100 and 500 feet above sea level.

Baltimore, once a small settlement, is now a leading city in the United States. People first settled this area of the Piedmont Plateau because of the abundant water. How is the water important to Baltimore now?

The waterfalls are important for two reasons. They provide water power and limit boating. Goods must be removed from boats at the falls. They are put on another ship above the falls or are moved ahead by trucks on land. The fall line is an ideal place for mills and to trade goods. For these reasons, many towns began on the fall line. Georgetown and Baltimore are two examples.

The soil and *climate* of the Piedmont Plateau are slightly different from the Coastal Plain. This makes it possible to grow different crops. Wheat, hay, and corn grow here. Many vegetables and fruits are also found on the plateau. The yearly temperature range is a little greater on the plateau than on the plain.

The Appalachian Region

The Appalachian Region is in western Maryland. It begins with the Catoctin Mountains near Frederick. It continues through the valleys and mountains to a high plateau. The valleys are well suited to apple crops. Most farms are smaller than in the other two regions. Lumbering is an important way of making a living in western Maryland.

At Deep Creek Lake, people can fish, swim, and play in the sand. This park on the lake's edge was made for tourists.

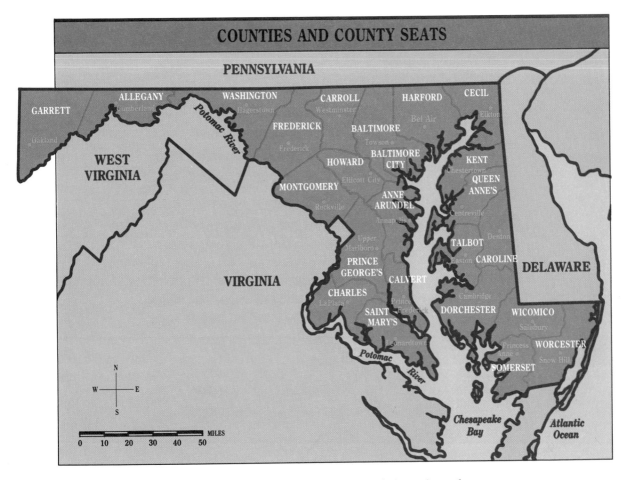

COUNTIES AND COUNTY SEATS

The elevation of the Appalachian Region is higher than the rest of the state. Almost all of it is more than 500 feet above sea level. The highest point is 3,360 feet at Backbone Mountain. Its height and distance from the large bodies of water keep the climate cooler than the rest of the state. There are no natural lakes in Maryland. Deep Creek Lake is manmade.

Political Features

Maryland has been divided into 24 governing parts. These are the 23 counties and the city of Baltimore. The sizes and shapes of the counties have been changed from time to time. This happened as groups of people wanted to separate from each other. Each county has its own government which is centered in a city or town known as the county seat. Many of the county names come from people and events in Maryland's early history.

Location

Being near the center of the first thirteen states of the United States has been good for Maryland. George Washington chose this central spot for the capital of our nation—Washington, D.C. At first, the capital was to be in parts of both Maryland and Virginia. Virginia's land was returned. Washington, D.C., is wholly on land that once was Maryland.

Many communities have grown near the tributaries of the Chesapeake Bay. These tributaries give transportation, power, and food. Baltimore, Washington, D.C., and Richmond, Virginia, are three of the largest of these communities. They are in the southern part of the East Coast *megalopolis*.

STUDY

WORDS TO KNOW

boundary

brackish

carnivore

climate

drainage basin

ecosystem

elevation

erode

estuary

fall line

fossil

founder

inaccurate

irregular

megalopolis

natural

navigate

omnivore

peninsula

plateau

pollution

survey

surveyor

tidal current

tributary

QUESTIONS TO ANSWER

1. What are the four states that border Maryland?

2. What is the boundary between Maryland, Pennsylvania, and Delaware called?

3. What percent of Maryland is land? What percent is water?

4. Name six things that act together to form an ecosystem.

5. Why are some of Maryland's boundary lines straight and others wiggly?

INTERPRETING WHAT YOU HAVE READ

6. Which river is saltier, the Severn or the Nanticoke? Why?

7. Which of the three regions of Maryland has the longest growing season? Why?

THINGS TO DISCUSS

8. If the maps used to decide Maryland's boundaries were being drawn today, might they be different? Why?

9. Which regions of Maryland would be nice to visit in summer and winter. Why?

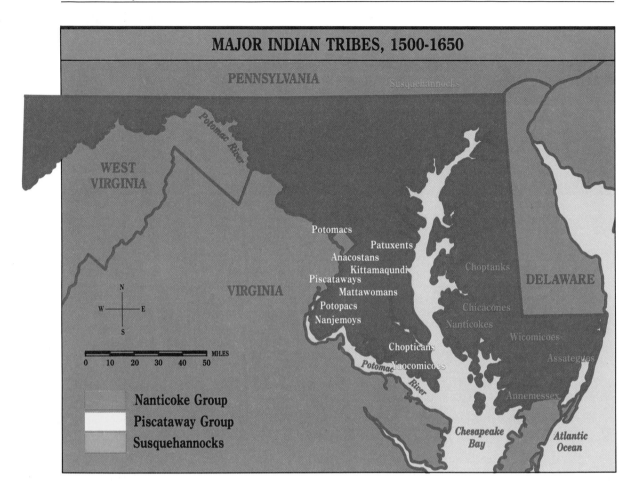

MAJOR INDIAN TRIBES, 1500-1650

PENNSYLVANIA

Susquehannocks

Potomac River

WEST
VIRGINIA

VIRGINIA

N
W — E
S

MILES

0   10   20   30   40   50

Potomacs

Patuxents

Anacostans

Kittamaqundi

Piscataways

Mattawomans

Potopacs

Nanjemoys

Chopticans

Potomac Naocomicoes

River

Choptanks

Chicacones

Nanticokes

Wicomicoes

Assateques

Annemessex

DELAWARE

Chesapeake
Bay

Atlantic
Ocean

Nanticoke Group
Piscataway Group
Susquehannocks

The First Marylanders

Who Lived Here First?

The first people to live in the place we call Maryland were Indians. Today they are called Native Americans. Almost all of the Indian tribes in Maryland belonged to the Algonquin nation. This Indian nation was made up of many tribes which spoke the Algonquian language. These tribes had probably been in Maryland several hundred years before the Europeans came. The Susquehannocks, who lived along the Pennsylvania-Maryland border, belonged to the Iroquois nation. They spoke the Iroquoian language.

Other Indians had lived here for thousands of years before the Algonquins and Iroquois.

How Indians Looked

What were the Indians like when the settlers first saw them? The Indians painted their bodies with colors made from roots and seeds. Sometimes certain kinds of copper and iron ore were used. Some people used paint for decoration. The painting could also tell something about the person. It could mean a man was a great hunter. A girl's paint might show whether or not she was married.

A Susquehannock
Indian brave as drawn
on a map made in
1608. The Susquehan-
nocks were a warlike
people. They often
attacked the Piscata-
way Indians.

The Indians living in Maryland had brown or copper-colored skin. Their eyes were dark. Their hair was black and straight. Some men wore their hair long. Others tied it in two bunches, called locks. The locks hung down the sides of their heads. Other Indians shaved parts of their heads. One side would be shaved so their hair would not get tangled in the bow string and arrow.

There was no reason for the colonists to be afraid of the Indians. The Piscataway Indians in Maryland were glad to have the English as friends. The Susquehannock Indians started wars with the Piscataways. The Piscataways wanted the English on their side. They thought the English guns would help protect them.

Women's Work

Men and women in a tribe had different jobs. The women had many duties taking care of the family. They cared for the children. They planted and weeded the crops. They gathered acorns and berries that were in season. They cooked the meals and made the clothing.

Indian women made earthen pots for cooking food. This picture made in 1590 shows how a large stew of fish and vegetables was made.

Sharp-pointed bones were used as needles for sewing. Thread was either strong, thin cord or dried and stripped animal muscle. The women made moccasins. These were soft shoes made from animal hides. Shoes were also woven from thin strips of tree bark.

Women also did *pottery* work. Clay was rolled until it looked like a thin rope. The ropes of clay were then made into rings and placed one on top of the other. Then they were smoothed together to make jars and pots of different sizes. The Indian women mixed shells or stones with their clay. This made the pottery very hard. Before the clay was dry, designs were pressed into the pots using cloth or rope. Then the pots were baked over a very hot fire. The Maryland Indians did not paint their pottery, as some other Indians did. Pots were used for cooking and to hold water. The women probably also made clay pipes. These were used by the men for smoking tobacco.

Men's Work

Men provided the meat and fish for the tribe. They hunted small animals such as wild turkeys, partridges, pigeons, rabbits, and squirrels. They also killed larger animals such as raccoons, beaver, deer, and bear. Ducks, geese, and many other kinds of waterfowl were hunted in marshes.

Fish, crabs, shrimp, eels, oysters, and clams were found in the rivers and the bay. A hook made of bone was fastened to the end of a line to catch fish. The Indians also speared fish. Another way to catch fish was in a trap called a *weir* (WEER). A weir was made by driving fence stakes into the river bottom. The fences had narrow openings in certain places. The fish would swim inside the fence and were caught because they could not find the way out. This way of catching fish is still used in some places today.

Men hunted for meat and skins during the fall. Their goal was to get enough food to last through the winter months. During the hunt, the men lived in small lodges. The lodges were made of saplings and pine boughs.

Indians traveled mostly by canoe. Making canoes was

This engraving shows a number of ways Indians caught fish. How many different ways can you see?

Diorama of an early Indian village from the Darnall Young People's Museum. The wigwams are covered with grass and bark. The village is surrounded by a wall for protection. The man in front is finishing work on a dugout canoe. Other men are just starting a canoe from the very large tree.

another of the men's jobs. Canoes were made from the trunks of large trees. One side of the log was set on fire. After it burned for a while, the fire was put out. Then the burned wood was scraped out with a clam shell. This process was repeated many times. Finally, only the shell of the tree remained. It became a canoe.

Indian Children

Indian children were never treated harshly. They were not punished or threatened by their parents. Children were taught how to behave by their grandparents, aunts, and uncles.

Naming a child was exciting for a tribe. Everyone helped name a baby. A girl would keep her name for life. A boy could change his name after his *vision quest*.

Children were brought up to believe in *supernatural* powers. Teenage boys went on vision quests. They were sent alone into the woods for a time. It was often a week or longer. The boys were expected to find their own shelter and food. They were to talk and listen to nature. If a boy saw a vision at this time, he could take its name. Perhaps he saw a wolf during his vision quest. He might then change his name to "Little Wolf."

Clothing

Indian clothing was made from animal skins. Deerskin was used most often. The skins were dried and softened to make clothes.

In winter the people wrapped themselves in long robes made of animal skins. They also wore leggings and high-top moccasins to keep warm. Hair or fur was left on the skins for winter wear. During the summer it was scraped off.

In warm weather adults wore little clothing. Children wore almost none. Both men and women wore something like an apron around their waists. They decorated their clothing with beads and *fringes*.

Men and women sometimes wore a few turkey feathers in their hair. A chief had a special kind of *ornament*. This was often a flat piece of copper fastened to his necklace.

Women sometimes tattooed designs around their arms and legs. To do this, they pressed sharp stones or bones into their skin. Dyes were then put into the cuts. The color remained in the skin after the cuts healed. White, green, red, blue, black, and yellow dyes were used. They were made from plant roots, clay, copper, and iron ore.

Shelter

People of the Algonquin nation lived in houses made from small trees. These small trees are called *saplings*. Two rows of cut saplings were placed in the ground. The tops were then bent together and tied with ropes. The ropes were made of

A longhouse of the southern Maryland Indians is under construction. This house is on display at St. Mary's City.

long grass or strips of animal skin. The framework was covered with bark. Grasses woven together were also used.

Most of these houses, called long houses, were the same size. They were about 5 feet wide, 10 feet high, and 25 feet long. The inside was one long room. Woven mats hung from ropes. These mats divided the house into several parts. When it was cold, a fire burned at the center of the house. An opening in the roof allowed the smoke to escape.

Long, low benches were placed along the walls of the house. The benches were made of tree limbs. They were covered with reeds and mats. These served as beds.

Villages were most often built near the water. This meant the Indians could get plenty of water and fish. In some villages the houses were scattered through the meadow. Other places the houses were built close together. A high log fence circled the villages. This helped protect them from enemies and bad weather.

Food

The Algonquin Indians got most of their food by farming. To get land ready for crops, the men had to clear the forest. They killed trees in two different ways. One way was to build a fire around the tree trunks. After the flames killed the trees, the leaves fell. The sun was then able to reach crops on the ground. A second way was to *girdle* the trees. This meant the bark was stripped all the way around the trunks of the trees. The trees later died, and over a couple of years, they rotted. The trunks could then be pulled from the ground by hand.

The women planted the crops. They planted beans, peas, squash, pumpkins, sunflowers, tobacco, and maize (corn). The women used tree limbs as hoes to break up the earth. High platforms were built in the fields for young boys to stand on. They were the guards. When a boy saw an animal or birds come to eat the seeds or vegetables, he would yell and wave his arms. This scared the animals away and saved the garden.

Indians gave part of every crop to the chief. He used the food when he hosted important guests. Food was always stored for winter. Sometimes food was buried underground in

A young Indian boy is keeping the crows away from the corn patch. From a diorama at Darnall Young People's Museum.

large holes that we call root cellars. Can you think why food was buried during the winter?

Some years the crops were poor. There was little food for the people. They had to eat anything they could find. Sometimes that might include their pet dogs.

Weapons

Indian hunters and warriors used bows and arrows, spears, and tomahawks. The bows were about five feet long. The wooden part of the bow was carved out of a branch. The branch came from an ash, hickory, or locust tree. The bow-string was made from deerskin.

Arrows were carved from lightweight sticks or hollow reeds. On one end was a sharp point of bone, horn, or stone. A few feathers at the other end helped guide the arrow in flight. Warriors and hunters were very good shots. Most were able to hit their targets on the first try.

The spears were like long, heavy arrows. The points of the spears were large, perhaps five inches long or more. They could also be used as knives. Spears were used when the men were close to the animals. Bows and arrows were used for

Tomahawks were used by southern Maryland Indians. These and other tools are on display at St. Mary's City.

killing animals from farther away.

The tomahawk at first was a simple wooden club. Later, a stone was tied to one end. The stone was ground and polished smooth. Still later, the Indians traded with the colonists to get metal axes. These were then used as tomahawks.

Tools such as drills and scrapers were made from rocks, bones, and wood. These tools had to be chipped, ground, and polished. This was done by rubbing the pieces with a very hard rock.

Indian Government

The Indians of Maryland had their own form of government. Each tribe had a council that handled the business. Each tribe had a chief, or *werowance* (WAIR-oh-wuns). A chief who ruled a group of tribes was called a *tayac* (TY-ak).

A *cockarouse* (KAHK-uh-rews) was another important man in the tribe. He was the war captain. He was also a member of the war council. A member of the peace council was known as a *wiso* (WEE-so).

The medicine man, or *shaman* (SHAW-mun), predicted things that would happen. He also treated sick people. He made ointments from roots, nuts, and berries. These were rubbed over cuts and spots that ached. The medicine man made medicine from bark, plant roots, or leaves. Medicine was sometimes served as a tea. The medicine man built the *sweat lodge*. This was a small, round building covered with mats. Inside, stones were heated. Water was poured over the stones to make steam. The Indians believed that an illness could be carried away by sweating.

A very important person in the tribe was the *orator*. He was the story-teller. He passed the tribe's history to the younger people through stories. The history was not written. The person chosen for the honor of story-teller had to have a very good memory.

A werowance as pictured in a drawing in 1590.

Religion

The Maryland Indians believed in a god. They called him Manito (MAN-ih-toh). They thought all good things came from him. The first food harvested from a crop was given to Manito. The first animals of the hunting and fishing seasons were also killed as offerings to Manito.

The Indians were frightened by a strong, bad spirit they called Okee. They offered food and tobacco to him. They tried to keep him happy so he would not harm them.

The Indians believed in a place like heaven. They believed that doing good things during their lives would earn them a place of happiness. By doing evil things, they would go to a place where people suffered.

Tobacco was used often in religious *ceremonies.* Indians blew the smoke over their bodies. They thought smoke would make them pure.

Indians lived in close harmony with nature. They depended on it for their living. They considered the earth to be their mother. They thought of animals as their brothers.

Money

The Indians used *wampumpeag* (WAM-pum-peeg), *peake,* and *roanoke* as money. These things were used by the Indians along the coast and made by the Nanticokes.

Wampumpeag was made from long strips of thick shells. The shells were made into a *cylinder.* A hole was then drilled through the cylinder lengthwise. The shells could be strung like beads.

Peake was like wampumpeag, only smaller. It was often strung like beads. Dark-colored peake was worth more than white peake. That was because only a small part of each clam shell is purple. It was more valuable because it was less common.

Roanoke was made from bits of flat shell that were also strung.

What does this picture tell us about early Indian life?

MERVIN A. SAVOY SAVES INDIAN WAYS

Mervin A. Savoy is in charge of the Title IV Indian Education Program in Charles County. Part of her job is to research the history of Maryland and the Piscataway Indians. She wrote a report on the history of the Piscataways.

Mrs. Savoy teaches arts and crafts to Native Americans of all ages. She also teaches dances and songs of the tribe.

Mervin Savoy was born in Prince George's County. Her background runs through several Indian lines. She is part Piscataway-Conoy, Cherokee, Susquehannock, and Nanticoke.

STUDY

WORDS TO KNOW

ceremony	orator	sapling	wampumpeag
cockarouse	ornament	supernatural	weir
cylinder	peake	sweat lodge	werowance
fringe	pottery	tayac	wigwam
girdle	roanoke	vision quest	wiso

QUESTIONS TO ANSWER

1. To what Indian nation did almost all of the Maryland tribes belong? To what nation did the Susquehannocks belong?

2. Name five jobs that were Indian women's work.

3. Name three jobs that were Indian men's work.

4. What was the Algonquin shelter called?

5. What group handled the tribe's business?

6. Who was the god the Indians believed to be helpful?

7. What did Indians use for money?

INTERPRETING WHAT YOU HAVE READ

8. What reasons can you think of for Indians thinking the earth was their mother?

THINGS TO DISCUSS

9. How does the work of early Indian women compare to the work of women today?

10. Make a list of foods that we know early Indians ate. Evaluate the list by comparing it to the four food groups that we study today. Do you think any food group was missing from the Indian's diet?

George Calvert,
first Lord Baltimore.

New Arrivals From Europe, 1620-1634

George Calvert, Lord Baltimore

O ur state was begun by George Calvert, whose title was Lord Baltimore. The king of England gave him the land which we call Maryland. It was a high honor for Lord Baltimore to receive such a gift. Let's learn his story.

George Calvert was born to a Catholic family in England in 1580. Elizabeth I was queen. She was also head of the *state,* or government, and church. The official church was the Church of England. It was very difficult for a person to get ahead without belonging to the ruler's church.

George Calvert's father wanted George to have the best chances in life. To help in this goal, he changed religions to join the Church of England. He saw to it that George was well educated. George attended Trinity College and studied law.

Queen Elizabeth died, and James I became the ruler of England. George Calvert became a close friend of the king and a member of his *council.*

Calvert, however, lost faith in the Church of England. He changed back to the Catholic church. That meant he could no longer hold a high office in the government. All people in government service had to take an *oath* of loyalty to the king.

If they did not belong to the same church as the king, they could not take the oath. George Calvert and James I were still close friends through all of this. The king gave George the title of *Lord Baltimore*. He also gave George a large gift of 2,300 acres of land in Ireland.

Charles I became the ruler of England after James I died.

Charles I, king of England.

Lord Baltimore Starts His Colony

In 1620 Lord Baltimore bought part of Newfoundland, off the coast of Canada. He named the place Avalon. He planned to start a *colony* that would make money. He also wanted it to be a place where Catholics could worship freely. Lord Baltimore invited a number of people to move there.

Queen Henrietta Maria, wife of King Charles I. The king's idea was to call the new colony "Terra Mariae." In Latin that means Mary's Land.

It was quite cold in Newfoundland. The growing season was not long enough for the crops they had planned. Lord Baltimore visited Avalon. It was so cold that he decided to move his group to a warmer place.

Lord Baltimore sailed to Jamestown in the Virginia colony, then on to England. After several tries, he persuaded the king to grant him land north of Virginia. Lord Baltimore agreed to name the colony *Maryland,* in honor of the queen, Henrietta Maria.

Maryland's Charter

The *charter* (set of laws) for Maryland was quite different from that of other colonies. Lord Baltimore had the right to rule the colony as long as his laws didn't go against the king's laws.

As the owner, Lord Baltimore could set up courts and collect taxes from the *colonists* (people living in the colony). He could also sell or rent land. He could make peace or war. The colonists would remain English citizens. They were allowed to trade with countries friendly to England. That was something the colonists from Virginia were not allowed to do.

This was the first time the people did not have to support a church with their taxes. The people of Maryland were free to attend the church of their choice. Baltimore's charter did not name an official church. Church and state were separate for the first time. This was a new idea. Maryland was the only colony to have such freedom.

Lord Baltimore II

Lord Baltimore's health had not been good since he spent time in cold Avalon. He died before the king's *seal* made Maryland's charter *official.* When a man died, his title and all he owned went to his oldest son. Younger sons were sent to school but *inherited* (received) very little of their father's wealth.

George Calvert's oldest son, Cecil, became Lord Baltimore II. He was now in charge of Maryland. The king of England granted him the charter for the colony in the New World. He was to pay the king two Indian arrows. He was also to pay one-fifth of all the gold and silver in the colony

Cecil Calvert, Lord Baltimore II.

each year on Tuesday of Easter week.

Virginia Worried About People Moving Away

The colonists in Virginia sent complaints to the king of England. They were afraid some of their people would move to Maryland where there were more rights and freedoms.

They worried for another reason. The king had allowed William Claiborne to trade on any land not already granted to another group. He started a settlement on Kent Island, which was inside the Maryland boundaries. Beaver hats were popular among the rich people in Europe. He was trading for beaver skins with the Susquehannock Indians. Claiborne got a high price for the skins when he sold them to traders from England. The Susquehannocks were a very warlike group and did not get along with many others. William Claiborne had a good working agreement with the Susquehannocks. Both he and they made a very good *profit* from the fur trade. Claiborne did not want the Maryland colony to have any of the beaver trade.

Beaver hats.

The D'orsay (1820).

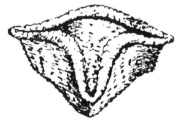

The Continental cocked hat (1776).

A clerical hat (1700s).

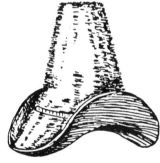

The Paris beau (1815).

Bringing People to Maryland

Lord Baltimore II planned for the colonists to leave England in the fall. They would arrive in Maryland in time to plant their crops in the spring. Lord Baltimore II decided to remain in England to protect the charter. His younger brothers, Leonard

Leonard Calvert was the first governor of the Maryland colony.

and George, were sent on the journey to Maryland. Leonard was chosen governor by Lord Baltimore II.

Large sums of money were needed to buy ships and supplies for the long journey. The settlers also needed to buy enough food to last until the first crops were harvested in the summer. To get people to *invest* their money in Maryland, Lord Baltimore II had an advertisement printed. Gentlemen investors were promised large pieces of land in exchange for paying the way for other people. Every five "head" of adult males brought over were worth 2,000 acres of land. Many of the interested gentlemen were younger sons who would not inherit any land from their fathers. They thought this was a great chance to be large landowners like their older brothers.

Inventory

When a man died, a list was made of all his belongings and their value. This was the law. There was a list of everything that was found in each room of the house, along with servants. Animals and food were also listed. These lists are called inventories. Inventories can be found in each county's records. They tell a lot about how people lived at that time. This record was also used in dividing the belongings among those who would receive an inheritance.

Why People Wanted to Leave England

In the early 1600s, many people were finding it hard to live in England. There were not enough jobs for all. Families were crowded together in small houses. The weather had been so bad that many farmers stopped growing grain. They turned their land into pastures for sheep. This caused a food shortage, especially for the poor. Many people went to the cities to look for a better way of life. Instead, they found poor living conditions and a lot of disease. People were eager to find a better life elsewhere.

Together, hard times in England and the handsome offers made by Lord Baltimore II got him the money he needed. Wealthy Catholic gentlemen were the chief investors. They signed *contracts* with poor people. The poor would work for a time in exchange for passage to Maryland. These workers were called *indentured servants.*

In England, poor people often worked for several years with little or no pay. This was the price of learning a skill or trade. As an indentured servant in Maryland, a poor person could expect to have a better life. Most of the passengers coming to Maryland were indentured servants. They were not allowed to marry during their term of service. Their contracts could be sold to another master.

The Jesuits, a branch of the Catholic church, also invested in the colony. This gave them a chance to teach their beliefs to others. They hoped to teach the Indians, whom they viewed as *savages*.

Most of the gentlemen were Catholics. Most of the indentured servants were Protestants. There were few women or children.

Indentured servant is sold during Living History at the Maryland Dove *dock. These people are part of a re-enactment of colonial life in St. Mary's City.*

Story of Coming to Maryland

One child on the first ship was 10-year-old William Browne. He was indentured to Thomas Cornwallis. He worked for Cornwallis until he was eighteen. Following is an imaginary *journal* written as if it were from young William Browne's viewpoint. Although Browne did not really write these words, the story is based on true information found in Father Andrew White's journal.

JOURNAL

November 1633

I, William Browne, am the youngest person on this ship. Thomas Cornwallis is my master, a very important wealthy gentleman. Governor Calvert and he are good friends.

So many barrels have been loaded below deck that I don't know where all the people will find room to sleep. The space is very small.

We started to sail once but had to anchor at Yarmouth, England.

22 November

Today some Catholic priests came on board. At last we are leaving England. The Ark is now on its way! Many people below are singing and praying for a safe journey.

26 November

Last night there was a frightening storm. I held on for dear life. The cries and screams chilled my blood. I had seen the Dove *sailing nearby. She had lamps on her mast, and then all was dark. I heard the sailors say "she's gone to the bottom of the sea." I am certainly lucky to be on this bigger, stronger ship. The sailors tell me it is large and strong enough to be in the king's navy.*

28 November

We, too, are sure to be lost. Another terrible storm has hit us. The mainsail has torn from top to bottom. We have been tossed by the wind and waves once more. Now all is quiet. I pray that we may survive. The crew is weary. The rest of us stay off the deck, out of their way. I don't raise my eyes to look over the side. Who knows what is in the sea?

Some of the gentlemen have wine, cheese, meat, and even live chickens. One of my chores is to take care of the chickens. I see the crew looking at them. *Those chickens had better stay alive until we reach Maryland. If not, Master Cornwallis will surely deal me trouble.*

December 1633

The lemons we must eat are terribly sour. People say we must eat them to keep away the sickness. The first mate says people's mouths swell up and they die. The sickness sounds awful, but so are these lemons.

My walking is getting better. I am more steady. Today I carried the pot of food up from the galley to Mr. Cornwallis and didn't burn myself once.

30 December

It has been weeks since we saw any land. The first mate says we have been going fast and should be at Barbados very soon. I should listen to him and not the wailing passengers below.

I thought this ship was so big. Now it has grown small. I can tell you everything about everyone on it. The cheese is gone from below. I am weary of eating biscuits and drinking beer. I miss my carrots and cabbage salad.

2 January 1634

When the Catholics meet it is quiet, and no one says anything about it. I see Father White writing in his journal every day.

Each night the captain of the ship and the gentlemen talk about the stars.

It is warmer now. I don't need to sleep under my heavy rug. I can sleep on top of it. We must be near the islands where we are to land first.

3 January

Land at last! The New World! It is very different. The people and the trees are strange. Even the Englishmen here at Barbados are very different from people at home. Some of the trees have no limbs, only a very tall trunk and huge leaves bunched at the top. It is very warm.

4 January

Miracle of miracles! The Dove has reappeared! How could it be? I wonder if Father White's prayers caused it?

It was my job to help soak and fill the water barrels. The cool water felt good on my feet. I haven't worn my shoes for weeks. They must last.

We sailed to other islands and took on some fresh food. I ate something new today. It was sweet and yellow inside, but the outside looked so queer. Larger than a turnip, it had prickly skin with leaves like knives coming from the top.

The Indians here are indeed strange. They have long, black hair and yellow-brown skin. They have

A crewman steers the Maryland Dove *as it sails in the Chesapeake Bay.*

many long, narrow boats. I saw a boy blowing a horn. The first mate said it was a shell. What a big mussel *must have been inside it. It was five times larger than shells I've ever seen.*

30 January

The crew told me stories of fierce, man-eating people—the Caribs—who live in these islands. They told of places on the land where water boils and rocks smoke. Can I believe them? I do not think I will leave the Ark again until we reach Maryland. I want to walk on land, but not if it smokes.

We have been on these islands four weeks. When will we arrive at Maryland?

27 February, 1634

We have come to Point Comfort in Virginia. The governor and three important men met with Captain Claiborne of Virginia colony. There are many big trees here and the river seems as wide as the sea.

5 March, 1634

We have finally dropped anchor at an island that Master Cornwallis called St. Clement's. There are birds everywhere, and I can see fish in the water. One island we passed must be the home for all the herons in Maryland. Some people will go ashore, and the women will wash the linens. The men are talking about going farther up the river to talk to the Indians about land where we will build our homes. Captain Fleet, who came on board in Virginia, will show the way. Maryland at last!

WORDS TO KNOW

charter	galley	journal	profit
colonist	indentured servant	mainsail	savage
colony	inherit	mussel	seal
contract	invest	oath	state
council	investor	official	

STUDY

QUESTIONS TO ANSWER

1. What were the two names of the person who began the state of Maryland?
2. Why did Lord Baltimore leave Newfoundland?
3. What new idea was put into action for the first time in the Maryland colony?
4. Who provided a lot of the money for bringing people to Maryland?
5. How did poor people afford to come to Maryland?
6. At what island did William Browne's ship stop to take on fresh water and fruit?
7. Where did the *Ark* finally drop anchor?

INTERPRETING WHAT YOU HAVE READ

8. How was Lord Baltimore like a king of a country?

THINGS TO DISCUSS

9. Why do you think wealthy Catholics invested in and came to Maryland?
10. If William Browne sailed from England to Maryland today, how would his trip be different?

*Leonard Calvert negotiated with the Indians for permission for the colonists
to settle in Maryland. Largely because of Calvert, the settlers enjoyed friendly
relations with the Indians. Shown with the Indians are Calvert, standing on
the* Dove, *Captain Henry Fleet, and a Jesuit missionary. This picture is
from a diorama.*

Maryland at Last, 1634-1700

4

Plan for a Town

L ord Baltimore's plan called for a town to be built. He hoped it would grow into a city like those in England. He wanted the houses close together and the streets marked off. This is one part of his plan that didn't work. In the very beginning, the houses were quite close together. They were either inside the fort or close to it. Within a few years, however, there was no need for the protection of a fort. Homes were then scattered along the waterfront. The colonists didn't need a fort in St. Mary's. They were friendly with the Indians.

Friendship Between Colonists and Indians

The colonists and Indians taught each other many things. They also traded. They got along well because they needed each other. The Piscataways were eager to have friends to help keep away the warlike tribes. These were the Susquehannocks to the north, Powhatans to the south, and Senecas to the west.

This friendship between the colonists and Indians made it easier for the Jesuits. Remember, they hoped to *convert* some Indians to the Catholic church. Father Andrew White kept a journal. He wrote about teaching the Piscataways. Kittama-quand, the Piscataway chief, and his family joined the Catholic church. The chief and his wife were married in a Catholic ceremony. The chief admired the ways of the English. He wanted his daughter to learn more from them. He arranged for his seven-year-old daughter, Mary, to live with Mistress Margaret Brent. Mary later married Margaret Brent's brother, Giles.

People of different races and religions lived together peacefully in the colony. *Religious tolerance* was a part of everyday life. Protestants and Catholics worked together to build the town of St. Mary's.

MARGARET BRENT

Margaret Brent and her sister arrived in Maryland in 1638 as free women. They were given some land by Lord Baltimore. Their place was named Sisters' Freehold.

Getting this land grant was very unusual. Margaret and her sister were able to own land only because they were single. If they had been married, their husbands would have owned the land. Margaret Brent later bought a plantation on Kent Island from her brother, Giles.

Freeholders often went to court to settle disputes. People would serve as their own lawyers. Margaret Brent did this quite often. She was skilled in court activities.

When Governor Leonard Calvert was dying, he asked Brent to take care of his estate, or belongings. She was a distant relative and good friend of the family. There were many bills to be paid. The governor owed a large amount of money to the soldiers who fought the Puritans. The men needed the money. They threatened to make trouble.

Brent sold some of the Calvert cattle to pay the soldiers. This kept the soldiers from making trouble and allowed the colony to go on in a peaceful manner. Lord Baltimore, the governor's brother in England, was unhappy with her actions. He did not forgive her, even though the Assembly wrote to him and explained why she sold the cattle.

Brent asked for a vote in the Assembly to represent the Calvert estate. She also asked for a vote for *herself, a freeholder. She was refused on both matters. The members of the Assembly came to her aid at a later time, however.*

Margaret Brent moved to

Virginia. There she spent the rest of her life. She was trusted by the Indian leaders and colonists. She was a sharp businesswoman at a time when women had few chances in that field.

Social Classes

The colony of Maryland had several *social classes* of people. In the highest class were the gentlemen investors. *Freeholders* were second. Although most of the freeholders were white, some were black. They were *freemen* who owned land and set up homes. Not all households were made of married couples. There was a shortage of women. Sometimes two or more men would make up a household. They would remain together until one of the men married. Freeholders could vote in the *Assembly*. This was the ruling body of the colony. Many freeholders later became large landowners and leaders in the colony.

Freemen were another class of people. Freemen were not indentured but did not have a household yet. Some came to the colony as freemen. Others had been indentured servants. Both black and white freemen worked to become freeholders.

Indentured servants were the lowest step of the social ladder. These people left the service of their masters as soon as they were able. At least one black man helped start the colony of St. Mary's. That was Matthias de Sousa, an indentured servant of the Jesuits. He came from Barbados.

People in different social classes would not have worked together if they had been in England. In the colony, though, they needed one another. People belonging to different churches worked together. People of different social classes worked together to make the Maryland colony strong.

Life on Kent Island

While people worked hard to build St. Mary's, William

Claiborne was very busy on Kent Island. In 1631 he brought settlers from Virginia to the island. He began trading with the Susquehannocks for beaver skins. The Indians got the skins north of Maryland and brought them to Claiborne.

It is not clear how many Virginians were on Kent Island. There were perhaps 22 people who worked there. These included an African, a clergyman, and a woman to do the laundry. They took livestock, tools, and seeds to Kent Island. They built a plantation called Crayford. There they raised corn and tobacco.

William Claiborne settled Kent Island.

WILLIAM CLAIBORNE, 1600-1677

William Claiborne was born in England in 1600. He went to college and was sent to Virginia as a surveyor in 1621.

Claiborne liked to trade and bargain. He set up two trading posts in the Chesapeake Bay. One was on Palmer's Island near the mouth of the Susquehanna River. The other was on Kent Island. Claiborne and his wife, Elizabeth, lived on Kent Island.

William Claiborne considered himself and his settlement to be a part of Virginia. Kent Island had been granted a seat in the Virginia Assembly in Jamestown.

When George Calvert decided to ask the king for land around the Chesapeake Bay, Claiborne got worried. He went to England to try to get the land for himself or Virginia. He failed, but kept trying. After the Maryland colonists landed, Claiborne tried to cause them trouble. He tried to get the Indians to attack the colonists. This did not work either. He did get Captain Henry Fleet to turn against the Maryland colonists, however.

MARYLAND'S EARLIEST SETTLEMENTS

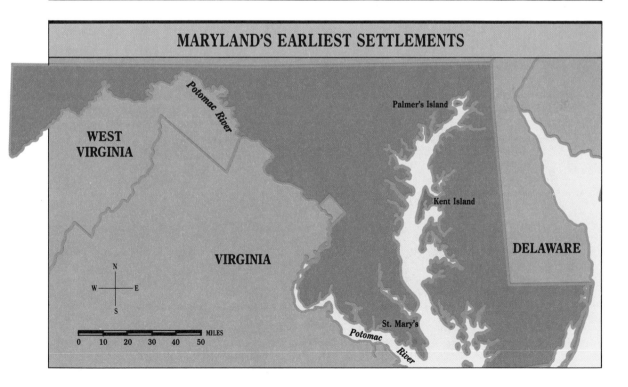

CAPTAIN HENRY FLEET

Henry Fleet came from Yorkshire, England, and began a real adventure. Although he came to the Virginia colony, he set up a trading post where St. Mary's is today.

Fleet was captured by the Indians. They held him for five or six years. When he returned to London, he received a lot of attention. One London newspaper explained that he had forgotten how to speak English.

Fleet said he had seen black fox fur (which was not known in England) and precious stones. He said the Indians sprinkled their paintings with gold.

Right away, there were investors willing to pay for Fleet's ships and supplies to trade for the fabulous riches he had seen. It is doubtful he ever paid back the people who paid for his adventure. He traded in London, New England, and the West Indies. Fleet also traded with Indian tribes across the eastern half of this country. They were good at making deals. Fleet knew their language. He also

Captain Henry Fleet showed Leonard Calvert a spot well suited for a colony. It was six miles form the mouth of St. Mary's River. Calvert traded the Indians axes, hatchets, hoes, rakes, and cloth for use of the land.

knew the land very well. He grew rich by trading.

Fleet was not altogether trusted as a businessman, however. He sometimes stretched the truth, even in his own journal.

Fleet had some trouble with the government officers in Virginia. They sent someone to arrest him. He could have escaped but chose to go back with them. When Fleet arrived in Jamestown, he said, 7,000 Indians were waiting with 40 skins each to trade. The people in Virginia were eager to be his partners in the fur trade. They let him go free.

When the Calverts moved their group to St. Mary's, Fleet was their guide and interpreter. He gave up his trading center so their village could be built. He explained to them what the Indians said. Perhaps Leonard Calvert offered to protect Fleet's fur trade business with the Indians.

Calvert gave Fleet 2,000 acres of land across the St. Mary's River from the St. Mary's settlement. Fleet built a house there and named it West St. Mary's Manor. The house was later sold to Thomas Cornwallis.

The Reverend Richard James started an Anglican church (same as the Church of England) on Kent Island. It was the first church built in Maryland. It has twice been moved. It is now known as Christ Church of Stevensville on Kent Island.

By 1634 there were about 100 people living on the island under William Claiborne's leadership. Craftsmen, planters, freemen, and indentured servants worked for him. Claiborne's small ship, *Long Tayle,* was likely built in a shipyard on Kent Island.

The Calverts of Maryland claimed Kent Island for their colony. Claiborne claimed Kent Island for Virginia. Lord Baltimore's men captured the *Long Tayle* and its crew. They were captured for trading without a license. A battle followed—the first navy battle in the colonies. The battle was fought in 1635 in the Pocomoke Sound. The Virginians on Kent Island surrendered to Calvert's men. After much talk, Governor Leonard Calvert took over the island in 1638. The people on the island were given a vote in the Governor's Council. Some people who now live on Kent Island can trace their background to that first group of settlers.

In the 1640s in England, the king was put to death. A group of Puritans ruled England. In Maryland William Claiborne and other Virginian Puritans took over. They did not allow religious freedom. Catholics were not allowed to be in power. During that time Claiborne sent Father Andrew White and the other Catholic priests back to England in chains. Father White's journal could no longer tell the story of early Maryland.

When Lord Baltimore got back into power in Maryland, Claiborne returned to Virginia. There he had a large plantation. He died in 1677 and was honored by Virginia.

Illness and Death

Thousands of people came to Maryland during the next 50 years. Many people fell ill and died within a few months of when they arrived. As a result, the *population* did not grow very much.

Malaria from mosquitoes killed some of the *immigrants* and left many others weak. They were too weak to fight off other sicknesses. Eating a poor diet and drinking *brackish* water added to their troubles.

Those who lived through the first several months had a good chance to live a normal lifetime. Until 1700 most of the people living in Maryland had been born elsewhere.

The colonists were not the only ones with troubles. The Indian population became smaller. Many Indians died from the new diseases brought over by the white men. Most Indian deaths were from smallpox.

Better Way of Life for Freemen

There were a few rich gentlemen and freemen among the new immigrants. Most were male indentured servants between ages 17 and 22. They had a chance to become freeholders by working four or five years. Once indentured servants became free, they often would work for someone else. Men needed money to have their land surveyed and ownership recorded in

court. Men were well paid for their work, mostly with
tobacco.

Freemen could also rent land. Part of the rent would be
paid by clearing the land and building a house.

Land was quite cheap, and there was a lot of it. Many of
the investors had only a small part of their land in use. Clearing the land and planting took a lot of work. It had to be done
by hand because there were few horses. Sometimes wealthy
men bought horses but used them only for riding.

Few women came to the colony. Only about one-fourth of
the immigrants were women. They could not marry until their
indenture was over. There were few married couples and not
many children. A large number of the children died of sickness
as babies. Families were quite small. Widows (women whose
husbands had died) married again very quickly. It was not
unusual for a woman to marry three or four times and have
stepchildren.

Tobacco, the Biggest Crop

The fur trade did not grow as expected for Lord Baltimore's
colony. The people needed another product to trade. Lord
Baltimore wrote very clearly that a field of corn was to be
planted for each person. He did not say they had to plant
tobacco. The Virginia colony had been growing tobacco for
years. Tobacco was the major item Virginia traded with
England.

The new people in Maryland began growing tobacco their
second year here. It quickly became their chief crop. Tobacco
was used as money in Maryland. It took hundreds of hours of
back-breaking work before a planter would get anything from
his crop. It would not be ready to trade for over a year.

The men in St. Mary's worked very hard. They built
homes and barns, raised crops, and hunted and fished. They
were always clearing land for more tobacco and corn. It was
soon a law that two acres of corn had to be grown for each
worker growing tobacco. In this way, Maryland built up a *surplus* of corn after the first year. The extra corn was shipped
to New England for sale.

Indentured servants working in the tobacco fields at the Godiah Spray plantation. These people are part of the living history in St. Mary's City.

The Early Homes

The early homes were very simple. They were usually made of wooden boards and had two rooms. They had a pointed roof and a fireplace. The roofs were made of straw or wooden boards like the walls. Some houses had a *loft* for sleeping. It could be reached by using a ladder. Most houses had dirt floors. The fireplace was very important. It provided heat for cooking and comfort. The chimneys were made with a wooden frame filled in with clay and small sticks. The same mixture of clay and twigs, called *daub and wattle,* was used to fill the cracks between the boards. It was common for the chimneys to catch on fire.

These pictures show the steps in growing and processing tobacco.

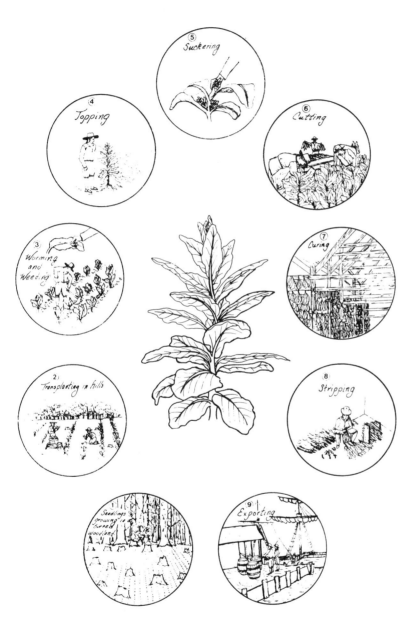

Illustration by Alice Webb

Planter's wife preparing a turkey to be cooked at the Godiah Spray plantation, St. Mary's City.

There was very little furniture. Making furniture took too much time. A rough table made of split logs was likely the first piece of furniture a family had. Benches were made in a like way. Large sacks filled with leaves or corn served as mattresses. They were placed on the floor. Bed frames with ropes to hold the mattresses would come later.

Cooking and eating were different from today. Wooden *trenchers* were used for dishes. They were often shared by several people. A trencher is a piece of wood with a hollowed place on one side. Food was put in the hollow. People ate with their fingers. A thick stew was served at many meals. Most households only had one pot for boiling food and one skillet for frying food. There were few knives. Forks weren't used at this time, even in England. Spoons were shaped from metal or from animal horn. The Indians taught the colonists to use gourds to dip water and stew.

In the beginning, everyone lived with little furniture. Later, the wealthy gentlemen, such as Thomas Cornwallis, had things sent from England. Their homes became more comfortable after that. As they could, people bought beds, chests, and dishes. They also had floor boards put in.

There were few household *utensils*. Candles weren't used before 1690. After sunset, the only light came from the fireplace. Some people used a simple lamp that burned fat or oil.

Women's Work

The woman of the house had many chores. She took care of the vegetable garden, cooked meals, and did the laundry. She also took care of the cows, chickens, and pigs. Sometimes she made the clothes.

Her garden was usually next to the kitchen door. It was called the kitchen garden. It was fenced in to keep the animals out. The woman possibly had only a hoe for a tool. She grew things such as cabbage, turnips, greens, beans, peas, and squash. Herbs were grown to season the food. Many of the

Inside an indentured servant's house there was very little furniture. The bed was on the floor and the chest held most of the person's belongings. Extra clothes hung on pegs on the wall. This photograph was taken at St. Mary's City.

herbs used then are now considered weeds.

Cooking meals took up a big part of a woman's day. She had to grind corn using a *mortar and pestle*. All cooking was done at the fireplace. This was a hot and dirty job. A woman had to be careful not to drop, spill, or burn the food. Any of these accidents would mean someone went hungry, because it took too long to prepare more food.

Food had to be *preserved* for winter. Root crops such as carrots, beets, and sweet potatoes were put in a root cellar. This is a large hole in the ground at least three feet deep. A thick cover kept the roots from freezing. Sometimes the root cellar was inside the house.

Milking the cow was one chore that women had to do every day. The milk and cream were separated. The cream was then used to make butter. People did not drink milk. Instead, it was made into cheese.

The livestock roamed free. They had to find food for themselves. Grasses, roots, and acorns were everywhere.

All the cooking was done over a fire. Do you think cooking over a fire would be faster or slower than cooking on a stove today?

Each owner notched his animals' ears. This mark would show who owned animals that were lost or stolen.

Washing clothes was another hard job. Women had to take their clothes to a spring or creek. They could also haul water back to the house and wash there. The women made soap from animal fat and lye. Lye was made from wood ashes. The colonists had few clothes, and they were not washed often.

Children worked in the house and the fields as soon as they were able. A child of ten or twelve years was expected to work like an adult. There were no schools at this time.

Clothing

Most people had only one set of clothes. They went barefoot whenever possible to save their shoes. The wealthy gentle-men had more clothes. Their clothes were also fancier. A traveling tailor would make the clothes if the woman of the house didn't. He would very likely be paid in pounds of tobacco or some other crop. The colonists needed all they had, so they didn't *barter,* or trade, things very often.

Religious Toleration

The people in Maryland had freedom of religion from the very beginning. This was part of their way of life. In 1649 the Assembly passed a law that said no Christian should be bothered because of his or her religion. Christians could not be forced to believe in a religion against their will. This law is called the Act of Religious Toleration. It was the first time anything like this was put into writing.

Several religious groups came to Maryland where they could worship freely. Some Quakers lived in Anne Arundel and Talbot counties. The Presbyterians were centered in Somerset County.

In 1660 King Charles II ruled England. He was not a Catholic. The Act of Religious Toleration was no longer in effect. Catholics could no longer worship freely. They weren't allowed to hold public office.

Government Changes

Charles Calvert became Lord Baltimore III when his father died in 1661. He made a new law. It said that only people who had 50 or more acres of land or who had a certain amount of money could vote.

Many freemen didn't have time to go to the Assembly in St. Mary's for one month. Instead, they gave their right to vote to someone else. That person would vote for them. This is called giving a *proxy*. Fewer men attended the Assembly. Most of those who did had the proxies of other freemen. (This was the beginning of an idea we use in government today. A few people in the Assembly represent many people in their counties.)

The Assembly was organized into two parts. The first was made up of *elected representatives*. This group included a chairman, or a speaker. The second group was made up of *councilors* chosen by the governor.

Saint Mary's is now an historic park. Visitors are welcome at this site of Maryland's first settlement and capital. There is a living history program that shows how Marylanders in the 1600s lived and worked.

In 1695 Governor Francis Nicholson moved the capital of Maryland to Annapolis from St. Mary's.

STUDY

WORDS TO KNOW

Assembly	freeholder	proxy
barter	freemen	religious tolerance
convert	immigrant	represent
councilor	loft	social class
daub and wattle	mortar and pestle	surplus
elected representative	plantation	trencher
estate	population	utensil
	preserve	volley

QUESTIONS TO ANSWER

1. What was the relationship like between the first settlers and the Indians in Maryland?

2. At least one woman was an important land holder in early Maryland. What was her name?

3. Name the four classes of people who arrived in Maryland from England. How were they different from each other?

4. Name the Virginian who first settled Kent Island.

5. What settlement was started by Leonard Calvert's group where Captain Fleet gave up his trading post?

6. Why didn't the population of Maryland grow very fast until the 1700s?

7. About what fraction of the early settlers were women?

8. What became the chief crop in Maryland?

9. What group of people took control of Maryland between 1645 and 1700?

10. What idea for government began in Maryland that we follow today?

INTERPRETING WHAT YOU HAVE READ

11. How would you describe the early homes of Maryland settlers?

12. What was Father White's contribution to the success of the early colony?

THINGS TO DISCUSS

13. How was Margaret Brent like the women of today? How was she different from most of the women of her time?

Packing tobacco into hogsheads at a plantation wharf. This engraving is from a map drawn in 1751 by Joshua Fry and Peter Jefferson. What can we learn about plantation life from this picture?

The Plantation

How Plantations Worked

The word *plantation* was used like *farm* is today. Just like today's farms, some plantations were much larger than others. There were many small plantations where the freeholder's family were the only workers. These freeholders were called *yeoman* farmers. Others may have had a few indentured servants or tenants. Some freeholders were successful and owned large farms. These men often had indentured servants, tenants, and slaves to work their land.

Today these very large farms are the only ones we still call plantations. Less than half of the white people of early Maryland were big plantation owners.

Tobacco plantations were large farms of hundreds, or even thousands, of acres of land. It took many workers to keep a plantation going. In the late 1600s Africans were brought to Maryland and sold as slaves. Plantation owners bought many slaves to work in the fields and help in the house. These workers were not paid any money. They were not given land after a certain length of time. The idea was that the slaves would always belong to the person who bought them. After slavery began, there were fewer indentured servants.

Many plantation owners began to trade with England on their own. They joined with other planters to form large trading companies. Others became partners with tobacco companies in England. Some planters even owned their own ships. Tobacco was shipped from plantation *wharves* directly to England.

Many plantation owners also became lawyers. Some won seats in the Assembly. Others were members of the Governor's Council.

SOTTERLY PLANTATION

otterly is a working plantation overlooking the Patuxent River in St. Mary's County. It can be reached by land or water.

The history of Sotterly begins in 1650. The land was granted to Thomas Cornwallis. The Plowden brothers bought it 50 years later. Part of Sotterly was sold to James Bowles in 1710.

James Bowles built the first part of the manor house *and* outbuildings.

The private front of Sotterly manor faces the Patuxent River. The breezes from the water made summer afternoons on the porch very pleasant.

An original slave cabin still stands. When Bowles died, his widow married George Plater II. They finished the manor house and other buildings in 1729.

Most of the work of building was done by indentured servants. Richard Boulton is said to have carved the shell alcoves. These are found on both sides of the fireplace in the Great Hall. Boulton also carved the Chinese-style stairway. There is a legend that goes with the stairway. It is said that when Mr. Boulton's term of indenture was over, he stopped right where he was. A short piece of rail moulding was still to be put on. Boulton put down his tools and walked away. There is still a gap in the rail—230 years later. Nobody knows for sure if this story is true.

Sotterly plantation has had many owners. Once it changed hands in a game of dice. The present owner, Mabel Satterlee Ingalls, has made the house a museum.

Manor House

Plantations were also called *manors*. The manor house was where the owner lived. These were huge houses. Brick was used on many of the homes. The rooms were large and had beautiful furniture.

A hallway ran all the way through the house to the back door. This was quite nice in the summer because it allowed a breeze to blow through the house. The hall was always cold in winter, though, because there was no heat in this part of the house. There were fireplaces in all the other rooms. A beautiful staircase led to the bedrooms upstairs.

There were usually two rooms on each side of the hall. These could be the dining room, sitting room, parlor, and library. The kitchen was apart from the house because of the danger of fire.

The sitting room was where the family gathered. The lady of the manor might sew there. She would sometimes invite neighbors for tea.

The parlor was the room in which guests were entertained after dinner. Chandeliers holding many candles lighted the room in the evening.

The library was the master's room. There he kept his books and business records, talked over matters with his plantation manager, and met with his ship captains.

The bedrooms were upstairs. Each bedroom had its own fireplace. Curtains were hung around the beds. This helped keep the people warm as they slept, because the curtains kept out cold air. Sometimes there were small rooms on the third floor.

Telescope House

Some manors had a *telescope house*. It was shaped like a telescope—small at one end and large at the other end. The reason is that is was built in stages. An owner would build the small end first, with a kitchen and another room. When he became wealthier, he would build a larger house and connect it to the first one. As his wealth grew, he built a grand house. This was connected to the second house. There are many telescope houses found in Tidewater Maryland.

Many manor houses could be reached by land and water. The "private front" likely faced the water. Often there was a meadow between the house and the water. They would have a

This telescope house is like those built by many Maryland planters. Which end of the house came first?

big, wide ditch dug. A fence was built down inside the ditch. No one could see the fence, but it kept animals out of the yard. This kind of fence was called a *ha-ha*.

The lady of the manor had her flower gardens at the private front. She also had a vegetable and herb garden near the kitchen. Different herbs were used as medicine, seasonings, and insect repellants.

Outbuildings

There were many other buildings away from the big house. These are called *outbuildings*. Tobacco barns were out in the fields. Each craftsman needed a small, separate building in which to work.

Clothing was made for everyone on the plantation. The workers needed several buildings for spinning, weaving, dying, and sewing the cloth. A building was also needed for the shoemaker. The candlemaker and soapmaker often shared a small building. Sometimes they worked outdoors. A smokehouse was used for smoking meat.

A rich planter's family even had a fancy "necessary," or outhouse.

A springhouse kept the milk and butter cool and sweet. It was built over a spring. Another low building was used to store ice for the summer. It was called an ice house. When the river froze in the winter, workers would cut huge blocks of ice. These were stored in a deep pit with the ice house built over the top. The ice blocks were covered with sawdust or leaves. This kept the ice cool, and it lasted well into the summer. Ice was only used for special occasions.

A washhouse is where clothes were scrubbed clean. A carpenter's shop was also very important. The carpenter was kept busy building many wooden items. He also repaired broken things. Wheelbarrows and carts were among the things he made. Another worker, a *cooper,* made barrels and buckets.

The carriage house, the stable, and the blacksmith's forge were often close together. The blacksmith made shoes for the horses. He also made pots and pans, nails, hooks, and hinges.

It was a great help to have a *gristmill.* There grain was ground into flour. Much flour was needed for baking. The gristmill got its power from a water wheel in a stream. Sometimes a windmill was used to make power.

A cooper often traveled from one plantation to another. He was highly skilled in making different kinds of containers. Some coopers made only buckets. Some made only barrels. Others made only hogsheads for tobacco, and a few coopers made all of these.

Schools

A most important building was the schoolhouse. Only boys attended school. Boys from several plantations would go to the same school. They studied basic subjects such as reading, writing, and arithmetic. If more schooling was desired, the young men were sent to Europe.

Public schools were built in 1723. In 1774 the free schools of St. Mary's and Prince George's counties were joined together. Their money went to build a school called Charlotte Hall. It opened in January 1797. Boys could choose to go to this school or attend school in Europe.

The Arundel Free School is the only known free school still standing. It is in Anne Arundel County outside of Annapolis.

Slave Quarters

The rest of the buildings on the plantation were slave cabins. They were very much like the first settlers' homes. They had dirt floors and a fireplace. There was no glass in the windows and very little furniture. Sometimes the cabins were built in one long row and attached to each other.

It took many slaves to do all the work on the huge plantations. If a master owned many slaves he hired an *overseer* to be in charge of them. The overseer was very important to the owner and had his own house.

Slaves who served in the big house lived in cabins nearby. The field hands lived in cabins closer to the fields.

The Plantation System

A large plantation was very much like a village. It was a business as well as a place to live. The owners had to keep records. Some of the old account books tell us much about life at that time. From the inventory made when a man died, it is possible to draw a picture of each room in the house.

ACTIVITY

INTERPRETING AN INVENTORY

Following is a small part of an inventory of James Bowles, who died in 1727. It is for one room in a house. Draw a picture of what you think the room looked like. Then discuss with the class what the inventory tells you about the person whose house it describes.

INVENTORY

In Madam Bowles's Room
6 leather chairs
3 old rush bottom chairs
1 old cradle, 4 pillow covers
1 large oval table
1 large looking glass, walnut frame
1 walnut chest of drawers
3 earthen punch bowls
4 cups, 3 saucers
1 large carpet
1 feather bed, blankets, quilt, sheets, etc. with curtains & valance
1 feather trundle bed & all furniture, sheets, etc.
1 pair andirons
1 pair fire shovels and tongs
1 chamber pot

Acres and acres of tobacco grew in the fields. It was hard, dirty work to raise a crop that would bring a high price. The owner's wealth depended on his tobacco crop. It was his money.

Black Slavery

Slavery began in Maryland in the late 1600s. Plantation owners bought slaves for several reasons. More slaves than white indentured servants lived through the first few months in Maryland. They were used to a hot, humid climate. They were given much cheaper food than the indentured servants. They could also work harder and longer than the English people.

Slaves became property. They belonged to the master for life unless he sold them to someone else. Any children and grandchildren born also belonged to the master.

Sometimes a family of slaves would have their own cabin. They would live as a family. These slaves were usually trained in household duties. The woman would work as the cook and her husband as the butler. Other members of the family served as maids, houseboys, and carriage drivers.

The family that worked in the house was luckier than the other slave families. The mother and father in the house raised and cared for their children. Families that worked in the fields sometimes were separated and sold to other masters. The children usually stayed with their mother. Uncles,

Slave cabin at Sotterly plantation. Windows have been added, but this cabin is much like it was in the 1700s.

brothers, sisters, or grandparents who lived on the plantation would help raise the children. Sometimes, though, there were no relatives to help the mother.

Care for Aged Slaves

A slave who was old, sick, or handicapped couldn't do as much work as a young, healthy person. An old one was worth little to the master. Many times the elders were not cared for. The lady of the manor house gave them their only medical care. Many men who had been skilled workers, such as blacksmiths or carpenters, were made field hands. Some masters refused to keep slaves who were old and feeble. Sometimes they were sold to buyers who did not know they could no longer work hard.

In 1755 one-fifth of all free Negroes in Maryland were either too old to work or were crippled in some way. They needed care. Some died of neglect. The Maryland Assembly passed a much needed law. It said slaves who were too old or sick to work could not be set free. The owners had to feed and care for these people as long as they lived. The owners were fined if they broke this law.

Friendship Chain

Some masters allowed their slaves to visit other cabins at night. The people would sing, dance, and talk. Other masters were not as kind, but some families still found ways to keep in touch with each other. They sent messages back and forth with other slaves who visited. It helped build a friendship chain that went from one plantation to another. A runaway slave could find kinfolk or friends. All along the route, slaves would help hide the runaway. With their help, sometimes the runaway escaped to freedom in the North or Canada. This system was called the *Underground Railroad*.

It was common for a husband or wife to travel 30 to 100 miles to see the other. They were cruelly punished by some masters if they were caught.

After the Revolutionary War, the buying of slaves from Africa slowed down. Blacks stayed on one plantation most of their lives. More of them lived in families. The black population grew.

Citizens Against Slavery

Slaves wanted to be free. They began to show this in different ways. Some worked more slowly in the fields. Others ran away or took part in *uprisings*.

People who worked for the freedom of slaves were called *abolitionists*. They wanted to *abolish,* or do away with, slavery. Abolitionists were both black and white, both women and men.

FREDERICK DOUGLASS, BLACK LEADER, 1817-1895

Frederick Douglass was born in 1817 in Talbot County. He was born a slave. During his youth, his master allowed another slave to treat Douglass badly. This and other cruel events made his life a very unhappy one.

As a teenager, Frederick Douglass's master sent him to Baltimore to punish him. There Douglass had to do back-breaking work on the docks. His job was to load and unload huge ships as they came and went.

Douglass wanted very much to learn how to read. While in Baltimore, he was able to do so, using a book on public speaking.

He ran away to Massachusetts when he was 21 years old. He took a job as a laborer *and was paid one dollar a day. He continued his educa-tion. Later, Douglass became a famous speaker and author. He started a newspaper called* The North Star. *He worked with white aboli-*

tionists but soon learned they didn't think Negroes were equal to whites. Douglass found he could no longer work with these people, for he believed all men to be equal. He continued on his own to speak out and write for equality of all people.

During the Civil War in the 1860s, he formed two Negro regiments from Massachusetts. They fought with the Union Army. (The Civil War will be covered more fully in chapter 12.)

Douglass still worked for the freedom of slaves. He spoke out, also, for the poor white people of the South.

Douglass visited President Abraham Lincoln to talk about slavery. He worked all his life for black people's freedom. He did not favor using violence to gain freedom.

Even though he faced many hardships, Douglass went on to become a United States Marshall. He also served as the United States Minister to Haiti.

Douglass lived in Washington, D.C., on an estate called Cedar Hill. Many people went to see him there and asked for his advice. In 1895 this great man died at the age of 78.

Many white people in Maryland did not like slavery. The Quakers were among these people. They were a religious group, many of whom lived on the Eastern Shore. Led by John Woolman, they decided to get all their members to free their slaves. Quakers who owned slaves were finally told to set them free. They could no longer be Quakers if they owned slaves. John Wesley, a Methodist, spoke strongly against slavery. In 1796 the Methodist church passed a rule against owning slaves.

Church members were not the only people working to stop slavery. Charles Carroll presented an idea to the Assembly in 1789 that would get rid of slavery little by little. It never became a law. It was one of the first times in Maryland that a well-known leader spoke out against owning slaves.

In 1789 some Baltimore citizens formed an abolitionist group. Samuel Chase was one of the group's officers. It finally broke up because it was so unpopular. Group members still gave money to a school for black children. Other groups, such as the Quakers, kept on with the job of helping slaves win freedom.

Some people in Maryland did free their slaves. The blacks were given a paper stating that they were released from service. These were called *manumission* papers.

The American Colonial Society worked to form a colony in Liberia, Africa, where Maryland slaves could return home. This idea was not favored by the many free blacks in Baltimore. It didn't turn out to be a very large colony, but today there is a state in Liberia named Maryland.

Some slaves overcame many dangers and hardships to win freedom. Harriet Tubman and Sojourner Truth are two black women who are honored for their courage and leadership.

HARRIET TUBMAN, 1820-1913

Harriet Tubman was born a slave on a plantation near Cambridge, in Dorchester County. She was one of eleven children. She was named both Araminta and Harriet Ross.

At the age of 6, she was hired out as a slave to James Cook. She was to learn the art of weaving from Cook's wife. Harriet also had to take care of Mr. Cook's underwater muskrat traps. The young girl caught pneumonia, likely from being in the cold water. She was sent back to her mother to be nursed back to health. Harriet was later hired out as a children's nurse. Many times she did not wake up when the babies cried. For this, she was beaten. Her back was *scarred from so many beatings.*

In 1844 Harriet married a free black named John Tubman. They lived together for five years but had no children. When Harriet heard in 1849 that she was to be sold, she ran away with two of her brothers. Her brothers turned back, but Harriet pressed on. She arrived in Pennsylvania as a free woman. She said she felt like she was in heaven.

Tubman did not forget the people who were still slaves. She made many trips to help others to freedom. She became a conductor on the Underground Railroad. She also became known as a spy during the Civil War. She secretly told the Northern army some plans of the Southern army. This was a great help to the North.

Harriet Tubman made many journeys back to the South. It is thought that she helped some 300 slaves to freedom. Her people nicknamed her "Moses."

A law was passed saying that slaves who escaped to the North could be caught and returned to their masters. Tubman then started taking her people to Canada. She would work until she had enough money to make another trip, then take more friends to freedom.

After the Civil War, Tubman helped many blacks get an education. She also started a home for the aged. She died in 1913 in New York at the age of 93.

The question of slavery was not to be settled for many years. Families were torn apart by their different beliefs on this matter. Brothers fought against brothers in one of the bloodiest wars ever known. The problem of slavery was not over until the Civil War in 1865. After that, the blacks were set free.

STUDY

WORDS TO KNOW

abolish	manumission	outbuilding	violence
abolitionist	laborer	overseer	wharf
chandelier	legend	telescope house	
gristmill	manor	Underground Railroad	
ha-ha	manor house	uprising	

QUESTIONS TO ANSWER

1. What were the huge tobacco farms called?
2. Where did the plantation owner live?
3. What is a telescope house?
4. Name five outbuildings that could be found on a plantation.
5. What was the work of a cooper?
6. What is a gristmill?
7. By what system were some slaves able to escape?
8. Name five people or groups who were abolitionists.
9. What black woman became a conductor on the Underground Railroad?

INTERPRETING WHAT YOU HAVE READ

10. How was a slave different from an indentured servant?
11. What did abolitionists do to help end slavery?
12. What can we learn about a plantation owner by studying his inventory?

THINGS TO DISCUSS

13. How is schooling today different than it was on a plantation in the 1600s?
14. How was a plantation like a small town of today? Compare government, services, and living conditions.

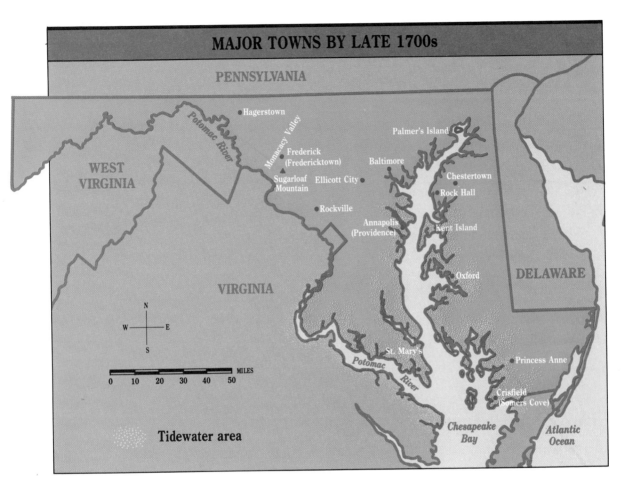

MAJOR TOWNS BY LATE 1700s

PENNSYLVANIA

WEST VIRGINIA

VIRGINIA

DELAWARE

Hagerstown

Potomac River

Monocacy Valley

Frederick (Fredericktown)

Palmer's Island

Baltimore

Sugarloaf Mountain

Ellicott City

Chestertown

Rock Hall

Rockville

Annapolis (Providence)

Kent Island

Oxford

St. Mary's

Princess Anne

Crisfield (Somers Cove)

Potomac River

N
W — E
S

MILES
0 10 20 30 40 50

Tidewater area

Chesapeake Bay

Atlantic Ocean

1700s Town Life Around the Chesapeake Bay

I n the late 1700s the population of the Maryland colony grew. The tobacco farmers needed craftsmen and *merchants* for supplies. Towns were started where there was a need for business and government. A few towns grew along the rivers. Annapolis was one of these earliest communities.

Puritans from Virginia settled in Maryland along the Severn River. They came because there was greater religious toleration in Maryland. Their little town was called Providence, or Anne Arundel Town. The Assembly changed the name of the city to Annapolis. This was done in honor of Princess Anne, who was to become the next queen of England.

Two Circles in Annapolis

Governor Francis Nicholson planned the city of Annapolis when he made it the capital of Maryland in 1694. He planned two circles in the center of the city. The two circles are State Circle and Church Circle. They were to remind people that the church and government (or state) were both ruled by the king of England.

The State House is the capitol building. The present State

View of Maryland's State House.

House is the third one to be built atop the hill on State Circle. Construction of this building began in 1772. The State House is the oldest capitol in steady use in the United States. Its beautiful wooden dome can be seen above all other buildings in the city. The dome was put together with wooden pegs, rather than nails. The building was made larger in the 1900s. The old part has been *restored*. The Old Treasury Building also stands on State Circle.

The Anglican Church of England was built on Church Circle. It was paid for by taxes until the colonies gained their freedom from England in 1776. The tax was often paid in tobacco. (Tobacco was used as money at that time.) The St. Anne's Episcopal Church seen there today is not the first one built there.

Town Problems

The major streets of Annapolis spread out from each circle like spokes on a wheel. They were made of dirt. There were open ditches and sewers. Cattle and pigs ran loose. Carriages and horses could be rented in the city. They were kept in the many stables there. *Sedan chairs* were sometimes used by ladies who didn't want their fancy slippers and dresses soiled by the messy streets.

Fire was always a danger because the only heat came from fireplaces. Many of the buildings were made of wood.

Fancy clothing worn by people in the cities during colonial days. Etching by James S. King.

This old fire engine was Annapolis's first piece of fire fighting equipment. It was called "Victory."

Fires destroyed many buildings in all of the early colonies. Annapolis bought a fire engine from England in the middle 1700s. The town also made a law on fire safety. The law said that two leather buckets must hang in the hallway of each house.

Work in the Town

Small businesses were built near the wharf. There were craftsworkers, merchants, and sailmakers. Ship chandlers sold groceries and hardware for ships. The wharf was the heart of the town. In the beginning, market days were held twice a week. Today, a market house is still there and is open every day.

The *Maryland Gazette* is the country's oldest newspaper that is still being printed. It was started in Annapolis in 1727. The *Maryland Gazette* advertised different kinds of businesses. Here is a list of some:

printer	blacksmith	milliner (hat maker)
goldsmith	cabinetmaker	seamstress
clock repairman	bookseller	tailor
cooper	shoemaker	music teacher
coach and	brickmaker	brass worker
carriage maker	dry goods merchant	barber
baker	grocer	peruke (wig) maker

In a restored part of Frederick, the storekeepers have hung signs like those of earlier days.

A sign hung over the door of each shop. The sign had a *symbol* to show what the shop sold. Many people could not read, so the signs helped them identify the businesses. A watchmaker would use a watch as his symbol. A tailor might use a picture of a dress or suit of clothes. One symbol still used today is the striped barber pole.

There were many indentured servants in the city until about 1700. A few black slaves also worked in the towns.

They served as house servants, carriage drivers, and *handymen*. Some learned other skills.

A postal system was begun in Annapolis. The postman was required to cover his route eight times a year.

WOMEN PRINTERS IN EARLY MARYLAND

Most people in the 1600s could not read. For this reason, there were few printers. In Maryland, however, three of the printers were women. That was very unusual for the time. Few women worked outside the home. Maryland's three women printers were Dinah Nuthead, Anne Green, and Mary Catherine Goddard.

Dinah Nuthead took over her husband's business when he died in 1785. She needed money to care for her two children. All she had was a printing press and a broken-down horse.

Nuthead moved her family to Annapolis from St. Mary's City. She got a license to print but was allowed only to print forms for the government. It is likely that she could not read or write. Perhaps she hired someone who could read and write to help her. There are many mistakes in the forms she printed.

Not much more is known about her. While she might not have been a very good printer, Nuthead showed courage. She did what she could with the only valuable thing she owned.

Anne Green took over her husband's business when he died in 1767. She became the publisher of the Maryland Gazette. *The* Maryland Gazette *came out every week.*

Anne Green tried to present both

This early printer's shop shows a cabinet where metal type was stored. Letters of the alphabet were kept separate. Words were put together in a wooden tray by picking out letters from the cabinet. Can you imagine preparing a whole newspaper this way? How long do you think it took to put together the words for one page hanging above?

sides of hot issues. This was very important just before the Revolutionary War. It helped Marylanders make up their minds about the war.

Mary Catherine Goddard's family had been in the printing business in Rhode Island and Philadelphia. She moved to Baltimore when her brother left the business. There she became the editor of Baltimore's leading newspaper, The Maryland Journal, *at the time of the Revolutionary War. Goddard is remembered chiefly for printing the first copy of the signed Declaration of Independence.*

Annapolis Was a Business Center

Annapolis had a busy harbor. It soon became an important business center for Maryland. A tobacco inspection house was near the dock of this bustling *port of entry*. The latest in fashion and household goods were *imported* from England. There were *ferry* boats to take people across the Chesapeake Bay near Annapolis. From Rock Hall on the Eastern Shore, people could travel on to Philadelphia and New York.

People from other parts of Maryland came to Annapolis to take care of their *legal* business. The Assembly and the courts attracted the leaders and rich people of the colony.

Annapolis As a Social Center

Annapolis was more than a business center. It was a social

Early Marylanders having fun inside the Tuesday Club. This drawing is from a history of the club written by Alexander Hamilton.

center as well. There were many balls and parties. There are
detailed records of several clubs. The South River Club still
meets in the same building club members used in 1742. Some
of the clubs were just for good times and good cheer, although
their members were well educated. The Tuesday Club and the
Homony Club were in this group. Other clubs met to *debate*
important ideas of the day.

Visitors to Annapolis could stay at one of the many inns.
In the winter, many rich plantation owners and their families
stayed in the capital city for the "winter social season." They
would often build a townhouse in Annapolis. This became their
second home.

A group of actors came through town to put on plays in
Annapolis. Many people also went to the race track.

Beginning of Public Education

In 1696 Governor Francis Nicholson offered his own money to
begin a school in Annapolis. The Assembly passed a bill that
established King William's School and planned a free school for
each county. King William's School is now known as St. John's
College. There was no money for the free schools until the
1720s.

Young men in Annapolis were taught by clergymen and a
few lawyers. Those who wanted a more formal education were
sent to Europe. Few girls were taught to read or write. They
were mostly taught needlework, manners, and dancing at
home.

Fine Architecture

Some of the country's finest examples of American *architecture*
are found in Annapolis. Part of the city is an *historic district,*
protected by law. Many buildings have been restored by a
group called Historic Annapolis. Each house had a garden.
Many had a stable for horses. Today visitors are welcome at
some of these buildings.

Annapolis never grew into a large city. That explains why
many of the old buildings are there today. Although Annapolis

This small brick building is the oldest public building in the state. It is the Old Treasury. When the colony's money changed from tobacco to paper, the money was issued here.

remained the capital of Maryland, another town was growing faster. Baltimore Town on the Patapsco River would become the new business center. It would also become a bigger port than Annapolis. In fact, it would become one of the busiest ports in the country.

Starting Baltimore Town

When present-day Baltimore was begun, there were already several towns with that name. There was a Baltimore Town on Bush River. There was a Baltimore Town in Dorchester County. There was also a Baltimore Town in St. Mary's County. None of these grew into large towns.

In 1729, 60 acres of land was bought from Charles and Daniel Carroll for a town. This new village on the Patapsco River was named Baltimore Town. It was named in honor of the Lords Baltimore.

Before 1729 this area had two small settlements – Cole's Harbor and Jones Town. At the time Baltimore was laid out, John Flemming already lived there. Jonathan Hanson lived just outside the town. He owned and ran a mill. David Jones also lived on the outskirts of town. Perhaps he named the town Jones Town and the falls Jones Falls.

Baltimore's Busy Harbor

Baltimore Town was popular for planters, travelers, and

By 1800 a town had built up around Jones Falls. The bridge seen in this painting was built in 1755.

traders. There were several reasons why this was so. 1) The Hanson mill was ready to turn its wheels and grind the grain people needed. 2) The Patapsco River had three broad branches and a deep harbor. The tide rose and fell only about one foot. Ship captains thought it was the best of all harbors. 3) Baltimore was also at a good crossroad. It was near the Great Eastern Road. This road came from Philadelphia and went on to Georgetown and Annapolis.

A bridge across the falls soon connected Baltimore with Jones Town. In 1745 Jones Town became part of Baltimore. Planters used the harbor to *export* large amounts of grain and tobacco to England. In return, they imported *manufactured* goods. Some of these were china, silver, glassware, and tools.

Germans Arrive

In 1734 a group of German people began to arrive in Baltimore. Daniel Dulany asked these people to come because they were skilled craftsworkers. They would help bring wealth not only to Baltimore but to all of Maryland.

The Germans were good farmers. They were also masters of many trades. Some worked in glass, pottery, bricks, and clothing. Others made leather goods. Still others were bakers, butchers, and carpenters. They started their businesses in Baltimore Town.

Baltimore Town first grew up around the waterfront. Beautiful homes were then built further inland. Over the years Baltimore has become a beautiful and busy *metropolis*.

View of Baltimore in 1752. About 300 people lived there. How is this view different from Baltimore today?

Chestertown

Chestertown was made the *county seat* of Kent County in 1698. It became the center of society and business on the Eastern Shore. Chestertown was very much like Annapolis was to the western shore of Maryland. Life was grand. People wore fancy clothes from England. There were a lot of parties and balls. Many people lived in beautiful homes. They enjoyed horse racing. Chestertown became a very busy and rich port on the Chester River.

Many of the *colonial* buildings still stand in the Historic District of Chestertown. Activities there help keep its history alive. Washington College, the first college named for George Washington, was founded there in 1782.

HORSE RACING

Horse races started in the early days of Maryland. In 1702 a law was passed against races on Saturdays. That was too close to Sunday, the Lord's Day.

Samuel Ogle and Benjamin Tasker started breeding horses. They were good friends. Ogle bought two English horses—Queen Mab and Spark. He brought them to Belair, his mansion in Prince George's County.

Letters and newspapers from the 1750s talked about the races at Annapolis. Many plantation owners raced their horses. George Washington came to the Maryland capital each fall and attended the races.

Today thoroughbred *horses are*

about three-quarters of Maryland's racing industry. Windfields Farm in Cecil County is the largest thoroughbred business in the state. Thoroughbreds race at several different tracks throughout the year.

Standardbreds make up the other quarter of the state's racing business. They are also called harness racers. They pull sulkies. One very good standardbred farm is Yankee Land Farm near Frederick. It is owned by Charlie Keller, who used to play baseball for the New York Yankees.

Horses are big business in Maryland. More than 12,000 people work in this industry. Feed suppliers, jockeys, grooms, trainers, veterinarians, blacksmiths, and cashiers are some who depend on the races for a living. The state takes in millions of dollars each year from taxes on betting.

Two of the biggest horse races in the country are held in Maryland each year. The Preakness is held at Pimlico Race Track in Baltimore in May. Preakness Week is a whole week of special events in the city. A blanket made of black-eyed susans, the state flower, is draped over the

This Currier and Ives print was a poster for a race held at Pimlico in 1827.

winning horse.

The Preakness is one of the three races that make up the Triple Crown. The other two races are the Kentucky Derby and the Belmont Stakes. Winning all three of these races is the highest honor for a thoroughbred in this country. Several Triple Crown winners have come from Maryland. They include Gallant Fox, Native Dancer, Kelso, Nashua, and Omaha.

The Laurel International Race attracts outstanding thoroughbreds from around the world. It is held in November and brings together thousands of racing fans from many countries.

Steeplechase races and fox hunts are also popular in Maryland. They are usually held by private riding clubs.

Oxford

Oxford was one of the towns planned by Lord Baltimore in 1683. Formerly its name was Williamstadt, in honor of King William.

Shipbuilding became very important in Oxford. Many ships docked at this town on the Tred Avon River in Talbot County. The town exported tobacco. It imported goods from England. One of the largest warehouses in Maryland was there.

Oxford, like Annapolis, stayed fairly small. Today it is a quiet town where one can still ride the Tred Avon Ferry.

Ownership of Maryland Changes Hands

Charles Calvert, Lord Baltimore III, died in 1715. His oldest son, Benedict Leonard, inherited the title of Lord Baltimore IV. He died two months later.

The fourth Lord Baltimore's oldest son, Charles, became Lord Baltimore V. Charles was only 16 years old and had to have some things approved by the king until he was 21. The Assembly, the proprietor, and the king got along very well. The Maryland colony moved forward.

The Tred Avon Ferry in Oxford carries cars and people across the river.

Charles Calvert, Lord Baltimore V.

WORDS TO KNOW

STUDY

architecture   county seat   export
colonial   debate   ferry

handyman	legal	restore
historic district	manufacture	sedan chair
import	merchant	standardbred
industry	metropolis	symbol
intersect	port of entry	thoroughbred

QUESTIONS TO ANSWER

1. Who settled Annapolis?
2. What do the two circles in Annapolis stand for?
3. Name two town problems in early Annapolis.
4. Where was the heart of the business town of Annapolis?
5. How did people who could not read know which shop to enter?
6. What unusual job did three women have?
7. Name the first free public school in Maryland. What is it called today?
8. Daniel Dulany invited people from what country to Baltimore?
9. What sport has been a favorite in Maryland since the early days?

INTERPRETING WHAT YOU HAVE READ

10. In what ways was Annapolis a business center?
11. Why was Baltimore Town a popular place for planters, travelers, and traders?
12. Of the three cities, Baltimore, Annapolis, and Chestertown, which two were more alike? Explain.
13. How were transportation and immigration important to Baltimore?

THINGS TO DISCUSS

14. If you were moving to Maryland in the late 1700s, which city would you choose as your home? Why?

*Old ruins of the Meshach Browning house built in 1828 at Sang Run,
Garrett County.*

Life on the Moving Frontier, 1700-1765

Maryland's Frontier

A *frontier* is the edge of a settled country. On the other side of the frontier is *wilderness*. Maryland had a frontier, as did every other colony. The frontier kept moving west.

In the beginning, St. Mary's was the frontier. The colony grew, and the Eastern Shore was settled. The frontier line changed to what is now Prince George's County and north to Pennsylvania.

The Tidewater part of Maryland had a large number of people. The land was nearly all claimed. As the soil wore out from growing tobacco, the fields were used for pasture and corn. New fields were cleared and planted with tobacco.

MARY AND MESHACH BROWNING, PIONEERS

M ary and Meshach Browning were two brave young pioneers in Garrett County. They attended school together, and in 1799 they married. After a day or two of celebrating, they set out on their own. Meshach traded his horse for a small farm with a cabin and several *acres of wheat. They had two plates; two knives, forks, and spoons; two cups and saucers; two tin cups; and a basket.*

The Brownings moved to Bear Creek Glades where their home was a partly torn-down cabin. On their first day there they killed two rattlesnakes, one inside and one outside the cabin. Mary had to scare away five wolves when she went to a nearby spring for water.

Meshach Browning wrote his story later in his life. He told of how he hunted many bear, birds, deer, panthers, wildcats, foxes, rabbits, and squirrels.

Mary took care of their eleven children. She also did many other chores to keep the family alive and well. She tended to the garden, milked cows, baked bread, and strained wild honey. She salted and dried meat. She boiled maple water into sugar, cleaned birds and fish, and dried berries. Mary carded and spun wool into thread. Then she wove the thread into cloth and made clothes for the family.

Their nearest neighbor lived three miles away. The Brownings moved about seven times. Mary and Meshach spent their last years in the small community of Sang Run. They were true pioneers on our country's very early western frontier.

Exploring Western Maryland

There have always been restless people who search for adventure and the unknown. Some of these adventurous men and women explored the western parts of Maryland. They found it to be a real wilderness. There were a few Indian trails and no settlements. Indians hunted in western Maryland. There were bobcats, bears, buffalo, foxes, and many other animals.

Explorers climbed Sugarloaf Mountain and saw the beautiful Monacacy Valley. They saw mountains to the west. This was the frontier. Lord Baltimore was eager to have the frontier between the Potomac River and the Susquehanna River settled. He made it possible for people to buy land there for almost nothing.

An early Maryland frontiersman who helped explore western Maryland was Thomas Cresap. He is known as Maryland's Daniel Boone. His home at Oldtown, near Cumberland, was on the far western edge of Maryland's frontier. Cresap made friends with the Indians and shared his meals with them. For this reason, the Indians called him "The Big Spoon."

Getting People to the Frontier

Around 1730 the German *immigrants* who settled in southern Pennsylvania were looking for more land. Virginia's governor made a very good offer of cheap land. Many of the Germans decided to go to Virginia. On their way from Pennsylvania they had to pass through the Monacacy Valley in Maryland. It had rich topsoil that was three feet deep. Most of the Germans didn't have money to buy land and didn't speak English. They didn't know how to get a land grant in Maryland.

Rich men in Tidewater saw a chance to make money. Daniel Dulany, Charles Carroll, and Benjamin Tasker were some of them. They bought much of the frontier land from Lord Baltimore. The men divided the land into small farms. Each farm was several hundred acres and was rented to the Germans.

JONATHAN HAGER, GERMAN FARMER AND LEADER

Jonathan Hager arrived from Germany when he was 22. He was a skilled gunsmith and blacksmith.

Hager bought 200 acres near the small settlement at Stull's Mill. In his first year there he built a stone house over two springs. It was built to be a very strong house that could serve as a fort. On the frontier it was not unusual for Indians to attack the homes of the settlers.

Jonathan Hager traded furs as

Hagerstown Courthouse and Square, 1776.

well as farmed. His home was used as a storehouse. He worked hard and quickly became a leader in the community. During the French and Indian War, he volunteered to be a captain of scouts.

Hager bought 2,500 more acres. He founded a town named Elizabeth Town in honor of his wife. Since most people called it Hagerstown, the name was soon changed.

Hager was the first German in western Maryland to serve in the General Assembly. He died at the age of 61 from an accident at his saw mill.

DANIEL DULANY

Daniel Dulany's life is one of Maryland's biggest success stories. He arrived in Port Tobacco, Maryland, in 1703. He was just eighteen. His trip was paid for by Colonel George Plater. Plater was a lawyer.

During Dulany's service to Plater, he worked as a clerk and bookkeeper. Dulany finished his four years of service in 1707. He studied law for the next two years. In 1709 he became a lawyer. He won most of his cases.

Dulany wanted to be rich. He saw the way to do this was to buy land. By 1720 he owned 27,200 acres. His land sold so well that a town was needed. Dulany named it Frederick Town. There he set up weekly markets so the farmers could sell their crops. This helped Frederick

Daniel Dulaney was important in helping to settle western Maryland. This engraving of him was made in 1755 by W. G. Armstrong.

become a trading center.

Dulany also started a spring and fall fair. He built a tradition that still goes on today. The Frederick Fair is held every September.

By opening western Maryland to the sturdy Germans, Daniel Dulany helped Maryland grow.

Frontier Farms

The land was settled quickly. Most of the settlers were German. There were also a few Scotch-Irish. Almost all were white freemen. There were a few indentured servants.

When a family settled in this area, they generally stayed in one place. Each family worked together on their farms. Slaves were not used by the German farmers. They raised more cattle than the planters in southern Maryland. Cattle didn't need as many workers as tobacco did. These frontier farmers were careful with their money and worked hard.

The German way of farming did not wear out the soil. The Germans used horses to help clear the fields of trees and stumps. This method was much different from the Tidewater farmers. The Tidewater tobacco farmers girdled the trees and let them remain in the fields. The Germans used horses to pull plows. The soil was hard and needed more than a hoe to *cultivate* it. Animal manure was used to keep the soil rich.

The Germans grew wheat, corn, hay, and *flax* as their chief crops. It took less time and work to raise a crop of these grains than to raise a crop of tobacco.

German Settlements

The Germans' settlement was different from the Tidewater settlements in other ways, too. The Germans' first homes were log cabins. It was not long before their homes had stone *foundations,* and some were built all of stone. Barns were used for cattle, hay, and storage. They were much larger than the tobacco barns of the Tidewater farmer. Many barns had stone foundations and were built into the side of a hill or bank.

With the smaller western farms, more people lived close together. They needed a trading center. Frederick became that center. *Craftsmen* and *professional* men soon moved their families to Frederick.

Frederick became a county in 1748. It stretched west from what are now Prince George's County and Baltimore County. Frederick was a very large county and was later divided into three parts.

ELLICOTT FLOUR MILL

Joseph Ellicott and his two brothers believed Maryland could become an important milling center. A mill is where grain is ground into flour. After looking for a good spot for their mill, they decided on the falls of the Patapsco River west of Baltimore Town. The water falls would turn a water wheel. This would make power for turning the wheels inside the mill where grain was ground.

The German farmers who grew grain in the Monacacy Valley and farther west could be customers. Charles Carroll, who owned thousands of acres, then began to grow wheat also.

Soon Ellicott Mills was well known. Milling became one of Maryland's leading industries at that time. Ellicott Mills became Ellicott City. The road from Frederick through Ellicott City to Baltimore became an important road. Flour was no longer imported to Baltimore. It became an export crop.

View of Ellicott Mills around 1850. Can you follow the route of the Patapsco River running through the town?

The Frontier Moves West

As more people moved west, other towns began to grow. Usually a large piece of land near a river and crossroads was purchased for the town.

An open space, or town square, in the center was the business part of the community. Hagerstown, Hancock, and Boonesboro each started this way.

The frontier had moved once again. It had moved past the Monacacy Valley to western Maryland.

From inside the block-house, soldiers could shoot through the small holes. It was very hard for an enemy to shoot the soldiers inside.

Forts

Past the frontier in western Maryland the settlers built forts to protect themselves against Indian attack. The Indians did not like white settlers moving onto their hunting grounds. Often a fort was just a small group of houses. A big fence was built around the houses. The forts did not have cannons.

Some forts had cabins, *blockhouses,* and *stockades.* Many times cabins formed one side of the fort. The outside walls were ten or twelve feet high. The blockhouses were built at the corners of the stockade fence. They stuck out past the outer walls of the stockades. Their upper floors were larger in every way than the lower floors. This left an opening where people on the second floor could shoot down on an enemy trying to climb the walls. Each fort had one very strong gate.

Ohio Company Explores

The Ohio Company was made up of rich men from Tidewater Maryland and Virginia. The company's job was to open settlements. They agreed to settle 100 families in western Maryland in seven years. They also agreed to build a fort and keep a small army there. The Ohio Company hired Christopher Gist to explore the wilderness. He was to keep a journal, draw a map, and report back to the company.

In October 1749 Gist arrived at a place called Will's Creek. It was close to what is now Cumberland. Gist followed Indian trails through the wilderness for several months. He made a deal with the Indians. They promised that the settlers could live in peace.

In 1750 the Ohio Company built a small storehouse at Will's Creek. It was stocked with goods to trade with the Indians. In 1751 Colonel Thomas Cresap marked a road from Will's Creek to the mouth of the Monongahela River. Cresap was one of the earliest settlers of western Maryland.

The land granted to the Ohio Company was also claimed by France. France was more interested in fur trade than in settling the land. The trading post at Will's Creek was attacked by some French soldiers. The post was destroyed, and the English traders were captured.

Washington Sent to Free the English

Young Colonel George Washington was called for an important task. He was sent to the French leader to ask him to free the English traders. On October 30, 1753, Washington set off on his dangerous journey. He had to pass through hostile Indian lands. Washington reached Will's Creek in November. There he hired Colonel Nathaniel Gist, a fearless pioneer, to go with him. They found their way through the wilderness. The French were unfriendly to them. The French would not give up the English traders. Things looked hopeless.

Washington returned with the bad news. The colonists knew they were in great danger. England also knew the danger and did not want to lose the colonies to France. The colonies had made a lot of money for England.

French and Indian War

Meanwhile, the French were busy building two forts. They connected them with a wagon road 21 feet wide. Because there were few French in the area, they got many Indians to help fight the English.

The French captured Fort Duquesne (dew-KAIN), which is now Pittsburgh, Pennsylvania. This began the French and Indian War in 1753. George Washington was at Will's Creek when he heard the news. He traveled to the mouth of Red Stone Creek to build a fort. He met some Frenchmen there, and the battle began. Several Frenchmen were killed. Others were taken prisoner and were sent back to Virginia.

After his victory, Washington began to build Fort Necessity. The French made a surprise attack. They overpowered the young colonel and his men. Washington's group had to return to Will's Creek. Washington left his soldiers there and rushed to Williamsburg to report how strong the French army was. The colonists in Pennsylvania, Virginia, and Maryland were surprised and alarmed at this report.

General Braddock Comes to Help

Orders soon came from England to build a fort immediately at Will's Creek. Washington was told that English General Braddock and 1,000 men would arrive to help them fight the French. General Braddock was well known. Everyone thought that it would only take him a few days to chase away the French. Braddock arrived at Annapolis. Governor Sharpe gave him supplies and news about the French.

Two things Braddock did would play a big part in the outcome of the war. 1) Braddock and his army moved very slowly. They built roads and bridges as they headed through the wilderness. This took almost three months. This gave the French time to build a large army. 2) Braddock had been told

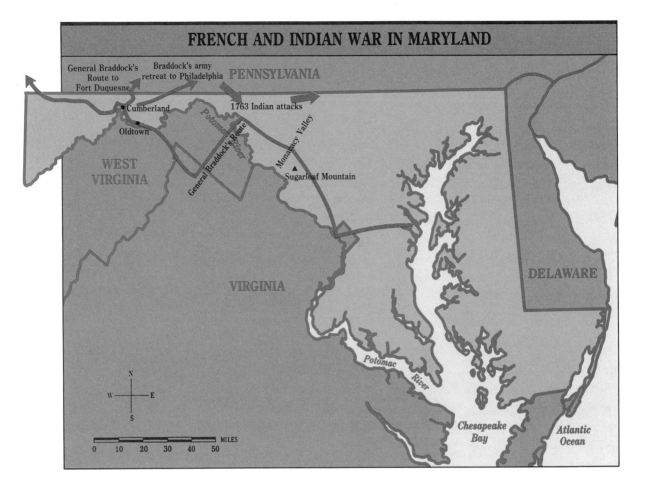

FRENCH AND INDIAN WAR IN MARYLAND

General Braddock's Route to Fort Duquesne

Braddock's army retreat to Philadelphia

PENNSYLVANIA

1763 Indian attacks

Cumberland

Oldtown

Potomac River

General Braddock's Route

Monakacy Valley

▲ Sugarloaf Mountain

WEST VIRGINIA

VIRGINIA

DELAWARE

Potomac River

N
W   E
S

MILES
0   10   20   30   40   50

Chesapeake Bay

Atlantic Ocean

how the colonists fought the Indians. Hiding behind trees and fences was not his way to fight. He thought it was cowardly. The European way to fight was in the open, and Braddock wanted to do that. He would not listen to anyone's advice. Later these two things would cause his defeat and death.

As they neared Fort Duquesne, the soldiers were marching in straight rows. They were all dressed in bright red coats with shiny brass buttons. General Braddock and his officers were riding on horses alongside their men. The officers were giving orders. They were sitting targets.

French and Indians Surprise Braddock

The French and Indian fighters had a clever plan. They surprised General Braddock near the fort on a level part of land with banks on both sides. One bank had a covering of thick, tangled bushes. The other bank was thickly wooded. About 500 Indians were hiding along these banks. The English could not see them, but the Indians could see the English very well. The English marched right into the trap.

The colonial soldiers had fought Indians before. When the firing started, they quickly took cover behind trees. General Braddock would not give the English soldiers the order to do this. They were shot down one after another. One by one, four horses were shot from under General Braddock while he gave orders to the men.

At last he gave the order to retreat. Almost at that very instant he was shot and killed. Half of the army was dead or dying. Colonel George Washington was one of the few officers who lived.

The retreat was a flight in terror. Washington led the Marylanders and Virginians out. An English captain led the few surviving Englishmen out of danger. They moved back to a place called Loyal Hanna. The French attacked several more times but were finally driven off. Loyal Hanna was safe.

Re-enactment of the Maryland First Regiment loading a cannon at Fort Frederick.

Fort Frederick State Park, Big Pool, Washington County. This is the last remaining British stone fort in North America. The fort was built in 1756 as a defense against the Indians.

Fort Duquesne Recovered

Winter was coming and the soldiers were tired. Some men were thinking of *deserting* the army. They wanted to return home. Just then a scouting party brought in three French prisoners. The Frenchmen told them that Fort Duquesne was very weak. The English decided it was the right time to attack. They did and overtook Fort Duquesne. The French had set fire to the fort before they withdrew. The English and colonial army repaired the damage. It was renamed Fort Pitt in honor of the prime minister of England.

French and Indian War Ends

In 1763 the French and Indian War was finally over. There were still many *skirmishes* on the frontier. Once the peace *treaty* was signed, people thought it was safe to move west.

Chief Pontiac Attacks the Settlers

Pontiac, chief of the Ottawa Indians, lived with his tribe on the Canadian border around the Great Lakes. He saw more and more Indian land being taken by the white people.

Following is part of a speech he gave to his Indian brothers:

"Why do you suffer [let] the white man to dwell among you? My children, you have forgotten the customs and traditions of your forefathers. Fling all the white man's things away. Live as your wise forefathers did before you."

Chief Pontiac went from tribe to tribe to get the Indians to fight. He did this very cleverly. None of the commanders of the western forts knew about it until it was too late.

Pontiac planned his attack for harvest time in 1763. The whole frontier west of Frederick became a bloody battleground. Many people were murdered in their homes and fields. Some settlers escaped to Frederick. Two companies of Maryland volunteers fought the Indians and finally chased them away.

The only good thing to come out of all this was that western Maryland was finally safe for settlement. The colony could now spread westward.

Chief Pontiac.

STUDY

WORDS TO KNOW

blockhouse	pioneer
craftsman	professional
cultivate	skirmish
desert	stockade
flax	treaty
foundation	volunteer
frontier	wilderness

QUESTIONS TO ANSWER

1. What is a frontier?
2. How did Daniel Dulany, Charles Carroll, and Benjamin Tasker make money in Tidewater?
3. Who founded Hagerstown?
4. What city became a trading center for people living in western Maryland?
5. What kind of protection did people in western Maryland have to build?
6. What was the job of the Ohio Company?

7. What event started the French and Indian War in 1753?

8. Who led the American troops during the French and Indian War?

9. Name the English general who was called in to help fight against the French. What two things helped cause his defeat?

10. What other group of people fought on the side of the French?

11. Who led the Indians in an attack on the settlers in western Maryland?

12. What was the result of the war?

INTERPRETING WHAT YOU HAVE READ

13. List ways the German farmers were different from the Tidewater tobacco farmers. Include their crops, buildings, and ways of farming.

THINGS TO DISCUSS

14. What personal traits and skills helped Mary and Meshach Browning survive in the frontier? Would those same things be helpful to people today? Explain.

This drawing of a riot shows how citizens felt about the Stamp Act. Can you describe what is happening in the picture?

Revolution and Independence, 1750-1780

Taxation Without Representation

The colonists had a General Assembly which was making many laws for Maryland. None of the thirteen colonies had representatives in Parliament, which was the law-making body in England. Some colonies had been paying taxes to England since the colonies began.

After the French and Indian War, England began to charge a tax. Many of the colonists thought this was unfair. The tax laws were being changed, and the colonists had no right to vote on them. *Taxation without representation* became a well-known complaint.

Stamp Act

The Stamp Act of 1765 was one new tax law. It said that all newspapers and legal papers had to have a special stamp on them. The colonists refused to pay for the stamps. They closed courts and newspaper offices. Zachariah Hood was the man in charge of the stamps. His warehouse in Annapolis was burned. Samuel Chase and some of his friends made an *effigy* of Mr. Hood. They paraded it through the streets and then burned it. Courts in Frederick opened again, but stamps were not used on legal papers.

England soon put an end to the Stamp Act. It took several months for the news to reach Maryland. During this time, groups called the Sons of Liberty formed in several counties.

WILLIAM PACA AND THE SONS OF LIBERTY

William Paca was born in what is now Harford County. His great-grandfather had come here as an indentured servant.

William went to school in Philadelphia. He was a very good student. He graduated from college when he was only nineteen years old. He left his family's home and moved to Annapolis. He studied law there with one of the best lawyers in Maryland.

It was not long before this handsome young lawyer married the richest and most popular young woman in town. He and his bride bought land on Prince George Street. They built the largest and grandest brick house in Annapolis. They had many friends and went to many parties there.

Paca and his close friend, Samuel Chase, organized the Sons of Liberty. Paca later served in the Continental Congress. On July 4, 1776, he signed the Declaration of Independence as Maryland's representative in Philadelphia.

Paca's wife had died, so he married again. Within four years, his second wife and two sons had died. Paca returned to Maryland with his two remaining children. He lived on a Wye Island plantation which had been left to him by his first wife. From the inheritances of his two wives and good money sense, Paca had become a rich man.

He was voted governor of the state of Maryland. Paca also served as a judge before he retired to his Wye Island home. He built another very grand house on the island. He died there October 13, 1799, at the age of 59.

More Taxes

Soon the colonists were required to pay more taxes. Business-men, merchants, and assemblymen got together and formed The Association. This group decided not to buy any of the goods that England was taxing.

At first the colonists stored taxable goods. They planned to sell these things when the law was changed. The law did not change right away, however. Ships carrying taxable goods were ordered back to England. They were not allowed to unload in Maryland. Then the law was changed once again. Now only the tax on tea remained.

Boston Tea Party

In many colonies the men were planning to *protest* the unfair laws. In Boston, Massachusetts, the Sons of Liberty dressed as Indians. They went aboard an English ship and dumped all the tea into the harbor. This was known as the Boston Tea Party. It caused more trouble. England closed the port of Boston. No ships could come or go after that.

Each of the colonies sent representatives to a big meeting in Philadelphia. They called this meeting the Continental Congress. They wanted to talk about how to deal with England.

The *Peggy Stewart*

During that meeting, something important happened in Annapolis. Anthony Stewart's ship, the *Peggy Stewart,* arrived in the harbor. In its *cargo* were seventeen packages of tea. Mr. Stewart paid the tea tax in hopes of avoiding trouble. The citizens heard about it and were very angry with Stewart. He offered to burn the tea at a town meeting. He printed an apology and had it handed out in the city.

Most of the people at the meeting felt Stewart's offers were satisfactory. There was still a small group of people who wanted more. Anthony Stewart was afraid of what might hap-pen. In order to save his life, he offered to burn the ship. He moved it to a spot where it could easily be seen. Then the

The Burning of the Peggy Stewart, *as artist Francis Blackwell Mayer imagined it.*

ship was set on fire.

Other towns in Maryland also had protests against the unfair taxes. Frederick and Chestertown have records of these events.

Continental Congress

The Continental Congress finished its meeting. The men suggested that the colonies stop trading with England. They still hoped to settle their troubles with England without war.

Two groups helped get Marylanders ready to face England. One was the Sons of Liberty. The other was a group like the Assembly, but it did not involve the governor. This group was called the Maryland Convention. Charles Carroll was elected to the Maryland Convention. He was a Catholic. It was the first time in many years that a Catholic had been voted to an office in Maryland.

CHARLES CARROLL OF CARROLLTON

Charles Carroll of Carrollton belonged to the famous Carroll family of Maryland. There were several Charles Carrolls who made news in the colony. Charles Carroll of Carrollton always signed his name that way to keep from being mixed up with the other men of the same name.

Charles Carroll studied law in Europe, staying there until he was 29. Law was not what he would have chosen for himself, but his father insisted that he become a lawyer.

When Carroll returned to Annapolis he was very busy taking care of the family's estates. He was not allowed to practice law in Maryland because he was Catholic.

His father gave him the 10,000-acre manor, Carrollton. After that, Carroll started calling himself Carroll of Carrollton.

He owned several racing horses. Soon he joined the Homony Club. He married a cousin, Molly Darnall.

Carroll wrote letters to Daniel Dulany that were published in the newspaper. The letters were signed "First Citizen." Many people learned that Carroll had written the letters. They liked his ideas. He became one of the four Marylanders to sign the Declaration of Independence.

Taking care of his family's land and serving in the General Assembly kept Carroll very busy. He was elected to the United States Senate in 1788. After his wife died, he moved to Baltimore to be with his older daughter. Banking and business took up most of his attention as he grew older. He helped start the Baltimore and Ohio Railroad. He laid the cornerstone of the railroad on July 4, 1828.

On November 14, 1832, Charles Carroll of Carrollton died in Baltimore. He was so loved by the people of the city that his funeral procession was much like a parade.

Revolutionary War

War between England and the colonies broke out in Massachusetts in April 1775. Two *regiments* of Marylanders left for Boston to help. They marched 550 miles over the rough roads in only 22 days. They didn't lose a single man.

Artist's view of the Second Continental Congress, held in 1775.

Second Continental Congress

The Second Continental Congress met. George Washington was made commander in chief of the Continental Army. He was well known for his part during the French and Indian War. The Maryland Convention organized the *militia* and printed money. Next it had to see that soldiers were trained and arrange for uniforms and weapons. A gun factory was built in Frederick.

At this point, the goal of the colonists was to win the right to vote in England's government. However, feelings against England grew stronger. The leaders sent by the king became very unpopular. Governor Eden made plans to return to England on His Majesty's ship *The Fowey*. The night before the ship left, six servants and one army *deserter* sneaked on board. The captain agreed to let them sail to England. This angered a group of citizens. The Sons of Liberty tried to remove the deserter but failed. They refused to let Eden's bags be loaded onto the ship. Eden sailed for England with only the clothes on his back.

Leadership in Maryland changed. No longer were the leaders only rich men. People began to think more about breaking away from England. The idea of being *independent* was gaining more support.

The Independence Question

Marylanders of the Continental Congress wrote to the leaders in Annapolis. They asked if they should vote for independence from England. Some people favored it, while others did not. The Maryland Convention was called to talk over this question.

On June 28, 1776, Maryland was asked to join with the other United Colonies. They *declared* themselves free and independent states. Four men from Maryland signed the Declaration of Independence in Philadelphia. They were Charles Carroll, Samuel Chase, William Paca, and Thomas Stone.

The Maryland Convention then decided to plan a new government for the new state of Maryland. Representatives would be chosen from each county.

SAMUEL CHASE, 1741-1810

Samuel Chase was born in Somerset County in 1741. He studied law in Annapolis. He was a brilliant lawyer and spoke out clearly on ideas. Chase was a great speaker. He could excite people with this speeches about liberty and independence. When the Stamp Act was forced on the colonists, he stole the stamps. He led parades in the streets and many other protests.

When George Washington became president, he chose Samuel Chase to be a justice of the United States Supreme Court. In 1804 Chase spoke so harshly of President Jefferson that he came close to being removed from the Supreme Court.

Samuel Chase was very fond of the time before the Revolution when he was a leader of the Sons of Liberty. Even though the style of clothes changed, Chase still wore his knee breeches, scarlet cloak, and three-cornered hat as he did before the war.

Samuel Chase as painted by John Beale Bordley in 1836.

THOMAS STONE

Thomas Stone was born in Charles County in 1743. He studied law in Annapolis.

Stone wanted to solve the problem between the colonies and England. He did not want the colonies to become independent. When war broke out, he changed his mind. This was a big step. The English wanted to capture the men who signed the Declaration of Independence. Stone and the other signers risked their lives for independence.

Stone also helped write the Articles of Confederation. He was elected by the Assembly to be the first governor of the new state of Maryland. Thomas Stone was on the committee from Maryland to plan the Constitution of the United States.

Thomas Stone was a quiet man who believed in solving problems without fighting, whenever possible.

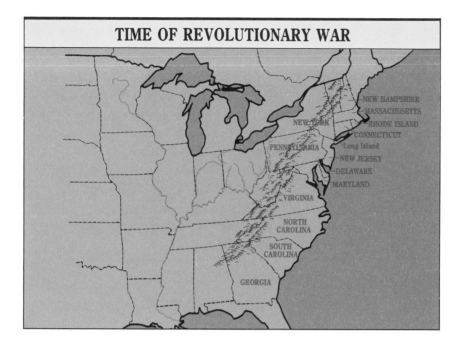

TIME OF REVOLUTIONARY WAR

Maryland Constitution

The Maryland Constitution was a plan for the government.
Not everyone could vote for representatives. Only freemen
over the age of 21 could. They also had to own at least 50
acres of land worth a certain amount of money.

Many freedoms were granted to the people of Maryland.
They once again had freedom of religion, as long as they were
Christians.

Maryland's New Government Begins

The new government met in the State House in February
1777. Thomas Johnson was chosen to be the first governor.
The new government also divided Frederick into three
counties—Washington, Montgomery, and Frederick. This gave
Maryland a total of nineteen counties.

Maryland Citizens in the Revolutionary War

There was very little fighting in Maryland during the Revolutionary War. Marylanders, nevertheless, played a big part.

Baltimore citizens built 250 ships. These were *commissioned* as *privateers*. A privateer was a ship that was privately owned by people, not by the government. The government gave these people the power to act for the country. The ship could fly the country's flag. It could raid other ships and take supplies. The goods could then be sold by the ship's owner. The privateers would have been considered pirates if they had not carried a license from their state or country.

Marylanders did many other things to help win the war. Farmers raised grain and cattle for the army. The state was an important supplier of cannons and gunpowder. Iron made in several parts of the state was used for weapons and tools. Women sewed clothes for the soldiers.

Maryland's Soldiers in the War

Maryland soldiers fought bravely in the Battle of Cowpens in South Carolina. The U.S. flag these men carried has been saved. This flag can be seen in the State House in Annapolis.

Maryland got its nickname "The Old Line State" from its soldiers' bravery. In the Battle of Long Island, New York, George Washington's men were nearly surrounded. Their only hope was to retreat. The Maryland line's job was to hold off the British so the rest of the troops could withdraw. The Maryland line was a *seasoned* group. General Washington called them "The Old Line." Of the 400 men, fewer than half lived. Only twenty were not hurt. Their brave deed earned them much praise throughout the states.

Several European generals came to train the colonial soldiers. General Pulaski and General Baron de Kalb helped train Maryland men. They are honored in our state today. General Lafayette of France helped organize supplies in Maryland. He also helped get France's aid to win the war.

Maryland War Leaders

Many Marylanders were leaders in the Revolutionary War. Among these leaders were Colonel John Eager Howard, Colonel Nathaniel Ramsey, General Otho Williams, General William

Smallwood, and General Mordecai Gist. They worked very
closely with General Washington.

JOHN EAGER HOWARD

John Eager Howard was a leader
in the army. The high point of his
career was reached at the Battle
of Cowpens. In this fierce battle,
seven English officers gave up their
swords to Howard. We have one
account in Howard's own words. He
said, "Captain Duncanson, of the
seventy-first grenadiers, gave me his
sword and stood by me."

In the war with England in
1812, Howard was again very active.
He was one of the men who organized
the Battle of Baltimore in September
1814.

Howard was more than a military leader. He had great wealth and
willingly shared it. He gave his land
for such great landmarks as Lexington Market, a Catholic church, the
University of Maryland, and the
Washington Monument.

He served as a delegate to the
Continental Congress. He was governor of Maryland from 1788 to 1791.
From 1796 to 1803 he was a U.S.
senator from Maryland.

Today there are several
reminders of John Howard. The
Belvedere Hotel on Charles Street was
named after his country estate.
Howard and Eager are two streets in
Baltimore named after this great
leader. Howard County is also named
after him.

Loyalists

There were people living in the colonies who wanted England
to win the war. They trusted England's government to rule
and protect them. These people were known as *Loyalists*. In

1777 all people in Maryland were asked to take an oath of loyalty to the new state. Those who refused to do so had a very hard time. If they stayed in Maryland, they had to pay three times more taxes than other people. If they left the state and returned to England, they lost their land and homes. Daniel Dulany was among those who returned to England.

Changes During the War

There were changes in many towns during the war. The people learned to make many of the things they once bought from England. More small businesses started. The new nation became independent in business as well as government.

England's General Charles Cornwallis surrendered to General Washington on October 7, 1781. This ended the war. The two countries then began to work out a peace treaty.

TENCH TILGHMAN

Tench Tilghman started his army career as a volunteer without pay. He later became George Washington's aide and a lieutenant colonel (loo-TEN-UNT KER-nul).

General Washington ordered Tilghman to take the news of the British surrender to Congress in Philadelphia. He left Yorktown, Virginia, on October 20 in a small sailboat. At Rock Hall he continued north on horseback. He traveled night and day and became very tired and ill. It was after midnight on October 23 when Tilghman reached Philadelphia.

A night watchman helped him. He delivered the message to Thomas McKean, the president of the Congress. The State House bell rang until dawn. The people woke and came into the streets to hear the news.

Colonel Tilghman arrived in Philadelphia on a borrowed horse without any money. Each congressman contributed one dollar to pay for his room and board while he rested. Later Congress voted to award him a horse, saddle, and sword.

Treaty of Paris

Maryland offered Annapolis as the capital of the new nation. Congress met there in the fall of 1783.

This painting is of George Washington resigning as commander in chief of the army after the Revolutionary War. It was reported that "there was hardly a member of Congress who did not drop tears."

Two important things happened during that time. Congress approved the Treaty of Paris. This was the final peace treaty between England and the United States. It was named the Treaty of Paris because *negotiations* (neh-go-she-AY-shuns) were held in Paris.

The second thing was that George Washington *resigned* as commander in chief of the army. He did this on December 23, 1783, in a speech to Congress.

Washington was the country's first hero and a friend to many people in Annapolis. The city honored him with a grand dinner and ball. A ball is held each year to remember him.

John Hanson was the first president of the United States in the Continental Congress, from 1781-1782. This was before the Constitution.

Articles of Confederation

The new states wanted an agreement among themselves. They still wanted each state to have its own freedoms, or rights. They wrote the Articles of Confederation. This became the new nation's plan of government. John Hanson, a Marylander from Frederick, was one of the leaders of the new government. He was elected president of the United States under the Articles of Confederation.

STUDY

WORDS TO KNOW

cargo
commission
declare

deserter
effigy
independent

Loyalist
negotiation
militia

privateer	regiment	seasoned
protest	resign	taxation without representation

QUESTIONS TO ANSWER

1. What was a major complaint the colonists had against England?
2. What tax law caused the burning of a warehouse and the closing of the courts and newspaper offices?
3. Who organized the Sons of Liberty?
4. What was the reason for the burning of the *Peggy Stewart?*
5. What big meeting was held in Philadelphia to talk about how to deal with England?
6. What war started between England and the colonies in 1775?
7. Name the four Marylanders who signed the Declaration of Independence.
8. When did Maryland's new state government first meet?
9. How did the new state government increase the number of counties?
10. Name the army leader who later gave land for the University of Maryland.
11. What were Loyalists?
12. What was the Treaty of Paris?
13. What was the name of the new nation's plan of government?

INTERPRETING WHAT YOU HAVE READ

14. Explain the difference between a pirate and a privateer.

THINGS TO DISCUSS

15. Suppose the Sons of Liberty were still around today. In what topics do you think they would be interested?

Congress Voting Independence, *engraving by Edward Savage around 1796.*

Maryland in the New Nation, 1781-1812

Settling Differences

There were many matters for the new country to decide. The Articles of Confederation did not set taxes or a form of money. Each state could have its own money. Each could tax imports and exports as it wanted. These differences caused trouble among states.

Maryland and Virginia were already arguing about something else. They did not agree on their boundary line in the Chesapeake Bay. Maryland, Delaware, and Pennsylvania were trying to decide who was in charge of the Susquehanna River and its connected waters.

Representatives from each of the thirteen states were invited to a meeting. The meeting was called to form a stronger United States government. Even though this meeting was held in Annapolis, Maryland did not send anyone to vote. Maryland did send *delegates* to the next meeting in Philadelphia. It was there that the United States *Constitution* was agreed upon. It is the plan for the government of the United States.

United States Constitution

The Constitution outlined a need for three branches of government. These are the *executive, legislative,* and *judicial* branches. It also planned for armed forces, money, and taxes.

The *Bill of Rights* was soon added to the Constitution. This protected the rights of each citizen. It gave Americans freedom of religion, freedom of the press, and the right to meet in groups. It gave other freedoms too. William Paca was one of the leaders pushing to add the Bill of Rights to the Constitution.

A New Capital City

The new country needed a capital city. Maryland and Virginia offered land for it. Many people wanted the capital to be in Pennsylvania where the government started. After much arguing, Congress decided it should be near the Potomac River. George Washington selected the exact spot. The site was a good one because it was near the center of all the states. It was also a gateway to the West.

A ten-mile square for the capital was surveyed. It was known as the Columbia Territory. Major Andrew Ellicott and Benjamin Banneker, a black, did most of the surveying. There were already two towns in the 10-mile square. Those were Georgetown and Alexandria. The capital city, Washington, would become the third town.

Pierre L'Enfant (pee-AIR lahn-FAHN) was chosen to *design* the city. He laid out the streets in a *grid. Diagonal* streets would be named for the states. Many wide avenues would be lined with trees and statues. Parks and squares would honor the country's heroes. It was a very grand plan.

L'Enfant had trouble getting along with the men in charge of building the city. He did not always have the different parts of the plan finished on time. Many different people bought land before the streets were laid out. One large house was partly built before the owner learned it would be sitting in the middle of a street. After much arguing, the owner had to tear down the house and rebuild it in a different spot. L'Enfant was fired. Major Ellicott was hired to finish the plan.

Benjamin Banneker's part in planning the city is not clear. Fact and *fiction* become confused. Banneker was quite old

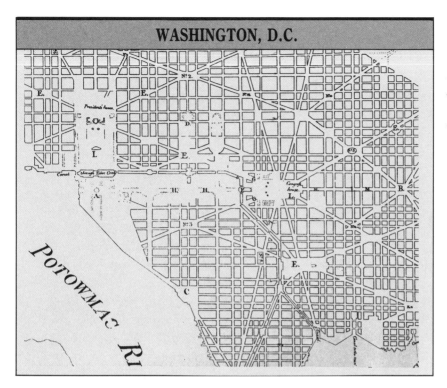

WASHINGTON, D.C.

This 1791 map shows part of L'Enfant's plan for Washington, D.C. Can you see the basic grid of streets?

when the city was planned. It is not likely he was healthy enough to do the work. It was remarkable in the 1700s that a free black man was hired to help survey the city.

BENJAMIN BANNEKER

Benjamin Banneker was born in Ellicott Mills on November 9, 1731. He was born free. He entered school at the age of six. He loved arithmetic. He would work for hours solving hard problems.

In 1761 Banneker made a large wooden clock. He patterned it after a small watch he had seen. His clock is said to have been perfect in every way.

Banneker loved nature, especially the stars. He would spend many nights outdoors studying the skies. As a result, he published an almanac in 1791.

His study of nature led him to discover that locust invaded the countryside every seventeen years. Banneker also learned that stronger hives of bees took honey from weaker *hives. He found out that weak bees were killed when they tried to defend their hives.*

President George Washington selected a group of men to plan how

the nation's capital would be laid out. Washington had read Banneker's almanac and admired his work. Banneker was chosen for the team. Washington, D.C., owes much of its beautiful design to Banneker.

In 1793 Banneker presented a plan of peace to Thomas Jefferson. Jefferson was the secretary of state at the time. Banneker's plan had four parts. It included 1) a secretary of peace; 2) doing away with weapons; 3) free education for the world; 4) no capital punishment.

Banneker was considered a genius. Many men changed their feelings toward blacks because of knowing Banneker. Banneker once told Thomas Jefferson that one God created all people. He had given us all the same feelings and the ability to think and learn. Banneker died a well-respected man in 1806.

Changes in People and Their Views

The law for voting rights was changed in 1801. Only free white males over age 21 could vote, but they no longer had to own land. The men did have to live in their voting areas for at least one year before they could vote. In 1810 the law about holding public office was also changed. Any voter could hold public office. Women and non-white people could not vote.

There were some people in the state who were against slavery. They felt it went against the ideas of both the Declaration of Independence and the U.S. Constitution. Ideas on this matter were presented to the Assembly several times.

This is a sugar bowl made at the Amelung glass factory.

Some of the ideas would have freed slaves over a certain age or would not allow any more slaves. These ideas never became law. Some of the leaders in the General Assembly helped form the Maryland Society for Promoting the Abolition of Slavery. Charles Carroll was in this group, even though he owned many slaves.

At this time, many people were moving to Frederick and Harford counties and further west. Some came from the worn-out tobacco farms in Tidewater Maryland. Many immigrants were coming to this country through the ports of Baltimore, Philadelphia, and Annapolis.

One immigrant was John Frederick Amelung. He was from Germany. He was one of the well-known artists of the time. Amelung started a glass factory near Frederick. He gave jobs to several hundred workers. Some of his work can be seen in museums today.

The immigrants were settling on farms and growing grain. More wheat was grown than anything else. Most of it was hauled to Baltimore by wagon. From there it was exported to Europe and the West Indies.

Conestoga wagons were used to carry people and supplies from one town to another. This wagon waits in front of a Baltimore inn. Why do you think it is there?

Transportation and Trade

Land *transportation* was still very difficult. There were very few roads in any part of Maryland. This did not matter as much along the southern and eastern shores. There, people got around by water. In the central and western parts of the state, however, there were fewer rivers and streams.

Hauling grain to Baltimore in a wagon was very hard without good roads. If it was muddy the wagon would get stuck. Wheels sometimes broke. The farmers did two things to help get around these problems. 1) They ground their grain into flour and 2) *distilled* it into whisky. Whisky and flour took less space than bulky bags of grain. Doing this also meant jobs for many people. Building and running mills and distilleries took many hands. Businesses began to grow.

Building Roads

Building roads took a lot of time and money. Trees had to be cut down. The stumps had to be removed. Bridges had to be built over streams. The earth had to be packed down hard. Rain always caused *erosion* of the dirt roads, so roads had to be repaired all the time.

Groups of businessmen in Baltimore formed road companies. They built roads leading west and north from the city. These roads were not fancy, but they were good enough to keep the grain moving to Baltimore. People in the harbor city knew that farmers might take their grain to Georgetown if there were no roads to Baltimore.

Everyone who used the road was charged a *toll*. This paid for the road. A long pole, or pike, was put across the road several feet above the ground. When a person paid the toll the pike was turned aside. The wagon could then pass through. These roads became known as *turnpikes*. The kind of wheels on a vehicle helped decide how much it would be charged. Because narrow wheels made ruts in the road, those vehicles had to pay more than ones with wider wheels. Sometimes people going to church were not charged anything.

Inns Were Important

Once people began traveling along the same route, inns were built along the roads. Everyone had to find a place to stay before dark. Each inn had a stable where horses were cared for and fed.

People arriving at an inn took whatever space was left. Many strangers would sleep together in the same room. There were no showers, pools, or televisions. Most travelers were men. They were often going somewhere on business. Women seldom stayed at an inn. Most women would only go to friends' or relatives' homes. If that could not be done, she would carry a letter of introduction. This letter said that the woman was of fine character. The letter was written by a clergyman and presented to a clergyman where a woman wished to stay. She asked to stay with the clergyman's family.

Inns became an important part of little communities. Men used them as meeting places. Those who were passing through town shared news at the inn. They would tell what had happened on their journey. Many times travelers or a

Fairview Inn on the Old National Road to Frederick. This painting from 1889 shows the traffic that followed the road from Cumberland to Wheeling.

stagecoach would carry letters. The letters would be left with the innkeeper until they were claimed.

Changes in Shipping

In 1798 Benjamin Stoddard was selected to be the country's first secretary of the navy. Stoddard had three warships built. One, named the *Constellation*, was built in Baltimore. It can be seen today at the Inner Harbor.

Baltimore, the largest seaport in Maryland, became the third largest city in the United States. The waterfront became lined with *piers* (PEERZ) and warehouses. They served the many ships coming and going.

New ships were built which were narrow and cut through the water very swiftly. These became known as the *Baltimore clippers*. Shipyards all over the Chesapeake were busy building these *sleek* ships.

Speed was very important because of the wars being fought at this time. England and France were at war with each other. Ships needed to move quickly and change direction when attacked by the enemy. Clippers could do this, but they did not hold as much as some of the larger ships.

Export Business

Men from Maryland sailed in fairly small ships to the West Indies. They exported tobacco to the islands. The men

This painting shows what a Baltimore clipper ship looked like.

returned to Maryland with sugar, coffee, and cocoa. Larger ships took grain and lumber to Europe. Trade was better than it had ever been.

A number of merchants became very rich. They were known as the *merchant princes*. They built huge homes and filled them with the finest *luxuries* of the time. They wore very fine clothes and invited guests to fancy dinners and balls. Some of their homes are museums today.

Religion and Education

The Methodist branch of the Episcopal church built chapels all over the state. The church had about 500 members in 1773. The Reverend Francis Asbury rode on horseback to preach in neighboring states. The Methodists separated from the Episcopal church on Christmas Eve 1784.

The Episcopal church, or Church of England, was reorganized after the Revolutionary War. It became known as the Protestant Episcopal church in this country.

THOMAS JOHN CLAGGETT, 1743-1846

Thomas John Claggett was born near Nottingham, Prince George's County. He studied with his uncle and then attended Lower Marlboro Academy. He went to college at Princeton. His height, six feet four inches, gave him an outstanding appearance.

Claggett became an Anglican priest and served in Calvert and Prince George's counties. He became a leader in the southern Maryland counties. Although he had been educated in private schools, he worked to establish Charlotte Hall. This was the first free school serving St. Mary's, Calvert, Charles, and Prince George's counties. The Maryland Gazette of July 21, 1814, tells us that he was elected president of a Bible society for Prince George's County. In this group were many well-known people of that time.

Reverend Claggett is best remembered for being the first American Bishop of the newly formed Protestant Episcopal church. He still served St. Thomas church in Croom while he was bishop.

JOHN CARROLL, CATHOLIC ARCHBISHOP

John Carroll grew up in Upper Marlboro in Prince George's County. He and his cousin Charles went to school in Cecil County and later in France. Carroll became a Catholic priest and returned to Maryland in 1741.

Before the Declaration of Independence, Catholics could not worship publicly. John Carroll traveled from

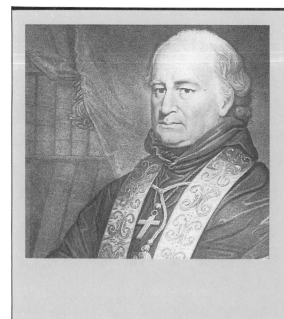

one private chapel to another to celebrate mass, teach religion, and help the sick and dying.

In 1783 at Whitemarsh Chapel in Bowie, Carroll and other priests began to organize the Catholic church in America. Six years later he was named bishop. He became the archbishop of Baltimore in 1790.

John Carroll had a goal of building a college for students, especially clergymen. He reached this goal in 1791 when Georgetown University was founded.

ELIZABETH ANN SETON

Elizabeth Seton came to Baltimore from New York to start St. Joseph's School for girls in 1808. In the first year of school she also formed the Sisters of Charity group which worked to educate girls.

The school and the Sisters of Charity moved to Emmittsburg in Carroll County. There Sam S. Cooper gave them land and money to build.

Seton was made the first North American saint of the Roman Catholic church in 1976. There are shrines to Mother Seton in Emmittsburg and Baltimore.

Washington College,
Chestertown, 1784.
This engraving is from
William Smith's
Washington College.
The building burned
down in 1827.

There were only a few Baptist churches in the state in the early 1800s.

Washington College was named for George Washington and was the first college in Maryland. It was founded in 1782 in Chestertown, Kent County. Several other colleges were started in the state. Some others failed to raise enough money to remain open or were destroyed by fire.

The College of Medicine of Maryland opened in Baltimore in 1807. It later became part of the University of Maryland.

STUDY

WORDS TO KNOW

Baltimore clipper	distill	luxury
Bill of Rights	erosion	merchant prince
capital punishment	executive	pier
constitution	fiction	sleek
delegate	grid	toll
design	judicial	transportation
diagonal	legislative	turnpike

QUESTIONS TO ANSWER

1. What were two weaknesses with the Articles of Confederation?
2. Name the three branches of government outlined by the U.S. Constitution.
3. What does the Bill of Rights do?
4. Who selected the exact spot for the United States capital?
5. Who helped survey the land for the nation's capital and also published an almanac?
6. What thing was needed the most to improve transportation for western Maryland?
7. What is a toll road?
8. Name three reasons inns were important.
9. What was the name of the new ship that was narrow and swift?
10. Name three church leaders who also helped start new schools in Maryland.

INTERPRETING WHAT YOU HAVE READ

11. "Fact and fiction become confused." What does the author mean by this statement?
12. Did the law for voting rights in 1801 allow for more or fewer voters than before?

THINGS TO DISCUSS

13. How is a traveler today different from one in the late 1700s?

The frigate United States *is battling the* H.M.S. Macedonian *during the War of 1812.*

War of 1812, 1812-1815

Countries in the War

The Revolutionary War ended in 1781. About twenty years later, England and France were caught up in another war. Other European countries also took part. The United States sold food and supplies to the countries at war. We were selling to both France and England. The merchants were making a lot of money by doing this.

Setting Up Blockades

In 1806 England began to station warships along the coast of France. Their job was to keep supplies from getting into or out of France. This is called a *blockade*. Countries cannot fight for long without food and weapons. The country that makes the best blockade often wins the war.

After setting up the chain of ships, England warned the United States. It would take over United States ships that were caught trading with France. France said it would do the same thing if the United States traded with England.

Running the Blockade

The Americans decided to *run the blockades*. That means they tried to sneak between the guard ships. This was very dan-

RUNNING A BLOCKADE

gerous. The Americans wanted to keep making money by trading with both countries.

England began to stop the United States' ships. American seamen were taken on board the English ships. England was looking for seamen with English accents. Anyone who spoke that way was thought to be a deserter from the English navy. Some of the sailors *were* Englishmen who ran away from the war. Many, though, were American citizens. At this time, many Americans still spoke with an English accent. The United States complained to England about this. England did not listen. The United States became very angry.

Americans Push for War

Many Americans wrote letters to the Congress about England. People in the West thought England was giving guns to the Indians. This caused trouble for them. They wanted to fight England for this. They also wanted to take over Canada. People in the South also wanted to go to war with England. Southerners thought they could take over Florida and maybe Mexico. (Spain owned Florida and Mexico at this time. Spain had joined the war on the side of England.) People in the New England states did not want to go to war. They were getting rich by shipping goods to England. They had fast ships that could easily outsail the French ships.

In Congress two men spoke for the people in the West and in the South. Their names were Henry Clay and John C.

Calhoun. They spoke in favor of more land. Congress was won over by their words and declared war on England June 18, 1812.

HAVRE DE GRACE

Following is a story of Havre de Grace as a youth might have written it.

My name is Billy O'Neill. I am a great-great-nephew of John O'Neill. He was one of a few men who fought the English at Havre de Grace in Harford County.

On May 3, 1813, the English attacked Havre de Grace. John O'Neill was stationed at a point above the bay. When he saw the ships, he and a team of men fired the cannons.

The other men got scared and ran away. They left Uncle John all alone. When he fired the cannon by himself, it rolled over his leg.

He went back to the town and joined another man, a Mr. Barnes, and they fought together. They tried to get the militiamen to help fight. Soon my uncle and some others were captured.

I read another account of this fight by Reverend Jared Sparks. He said that when Uncle John was taken

What is happening in this picture of the burning of Havre de Grace?

prisoner he had two muskets in his hand but had no ammunition. He surely was a brave man, wasn't he?

Well, the English weren't happy with just firing their cannons into the town. They went into every house and took anything they wanted. They used axes on doors, chests, and locked closets. Officers wrote their names on items they wanted. Then they had their soldiers take the goods to the ships.

The English stayed only four hours but burned 49 of the 60 homes in Havre de Grace. All of the homes were damaged in some way. Most of the people had to rebuild. But they all worked together and met the task.

When I read my uncle's account of this attack, I was angry and sad. Havre de Grace is beautiful. Havre de Grace means harbor of beauty. I hope it will always remain this way.

ST. MICHAEL'S STORY

The town of St. Michael's knew the English were planning to attack. The people built a fort and placed logs and chains across the entrance of the harbor. Brigadier General Perry Benson was in charge of the Maryland militia. As night came, he had his men place lanterns in the tops of the tallest trees and on the high masts of boats in the harbor. All other lights in the town were put out.

The English marines came ashore after midnight. The gunners at the fort were ready. They fired two cannons at the advancing troops. There was no time to reload the cannons. The defenders grabbed their flag and ran to join the others in St. Michael's.

Many of the English marines were killed or wounded by the cannon fire. The rest went back to their ship. The English then aimed their cannons at the lights on the shore. They fired. The lights in the trees and on the tall ships caused the English to shoot over the houses. Little harm was done to St. Michael's. The blackout helped confuse the enemy in battle.

There is a house on Main Street in St. Michael's known as the Cannon Ball House. It still stands just as it did during the English attack. A cannon ball crashed through the wall of the house during the attack. It rolled down the stairs right past a woman holding a child. Nobody in the town was killed or hurt in the attack.

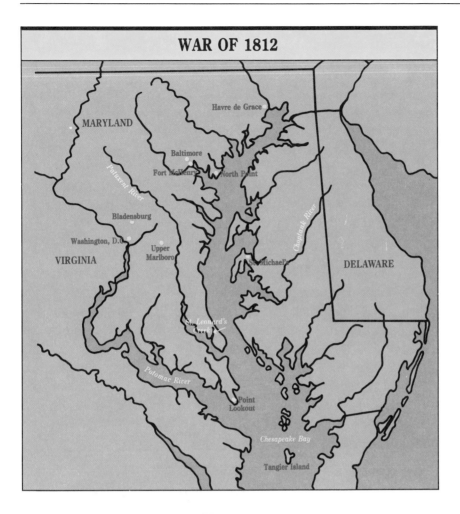

WAR OF 1812

United States Navy Goes to War

The United States marched upon Canada first. A little village
called York was attacked and burned. York is now known as
Toronto. This was the only battle Americans won in Canada.
The Americans won battles on Lake Erie and Lake Champlain.
This kept the English from entering the United States from
the north.

The United States began the war with about fifteen ships.
England's navy had 830 ships, though most were busy fighting
France. The Americans built ships quickly. Many were built in
little towns along the Chesapeake Bay. The ships were fast

and easy to *maneuver*. The *Constitution* was one ship to sail out of the Chesapeake Bay. It fought one of England's best ships, the *Guerriere*. The English had never seen a ship like the *Constitution*. They laughed, but the *Constitution* caught the *Guerriere* and won after a 30-minute battle. The *Constitution* was called "Old Ironsides" after the battle. Later a poem was written about it. Many other English ships were captured or sunk. England began to take the United States seriously.

More and more merchant ships were built with cannons. They were made privateers. The English called them pirates. They called Baltimore the "Pirates' Den."

Navy Leader Joshua Barney

Joshua Barney was a brave officer of the Revolutionary War. He was asked to command a *flotilla* (flo-TIL-uh) of gunboats which were being built in Baltimore. The little group of boats would not be part of the U.S. Navy, but they would take orders from the national government.

In April 1814 Commodore Barney set out for Tangier Island. Tangier Island had been taken over by the English. Barney sailed out of the Patuxent River. A large group of English ships pushed him back. The flotilla was blockaded. The big enemy chased after the little American ships as far as St.

Joshua Barney.

Leonard's Creek. Then smaller English boats were sent to fight. The English stayed and fought for three days before retreating. The flotilla's guns were no match for the English warships. Even so, the 500 men on the U.S. boats fought bravely. They kept back the large English force.

Commodore Barney decided to destroy his boats. He didn't want the English to take them over. Barney and his men burned and sank the boats near Upper Marlboro in Prince George's County. Then they marched to Washington, D.C., to help defend the capital city.

Battle at Washington, D.C.

Again, the poorly-trained militia had to fight the well-trained English army. Barney and his men helped the militia. The two armies met at Bladensburg, near Washington. The Americans fought very poorly. Many militiamen threw down their guns and ran away. For that reason, some people call the battle the "Bladensburg Races."

Barney and his men held their ground. Barney was wounded in the battle. He ordered his men to retreat without him. The English knew of Barney's brave fight on the Patuxent. When the English leaders learned he had been wounded, they arranged for him to be treated. Barney was carried to safety.

The English troops moved on to Washington. They set fire to the Capitol, the White House, and several other buildings. They burned Washington because it was the capital of the United States and because the Americans had burned York in Canada. President James Madison's wife, Dolly, saved some things from the White House. One was a painting of George Washington.

Battle at Baltimore

The English thought Baltimore was a pirates' nest. They planned to burn the city. They were in for a big surprise. Baltimore was ready for them. The people of Baltimore worked together. They were determined not to let the English land. A huge flag was flying over Fort McHenry. The flag was made by Mary Pickersgill. Her house is known today as the Flag House.

General John Stricker and 3,000 Baltimore soldiers were sent to do a task—slow down the English. They were sent to North Point to find out how many English soldiers there were. Stricker's men also were to learn the English battle plan.

The two armies met. The Americans fought stubbornly for awhile. Then they began to slowly withdraw toward Baltimore. They *felled* trees along the road to slow the English. There were several other reasons why the English followed slowly. General Ross, whom they liked very much, had been killed. They felt badly about his death. The weather was also very hot and rainy.

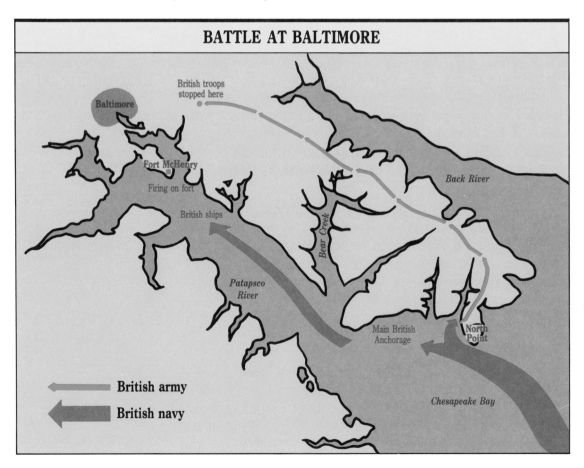

BATTLE AT BALTIMORE

Assembly of the Troops Before Baltimore, *1814. The painting is by Thomas C. Ruckle. Why do you think the gentlemen in top hats are there?*

The English arrived at Baltimore. They were surprised at what they saw. There were 12,000 soldiers and many cannons facing them. The English soldiers sent word to their ships that they needed help.

Many English ships were sunk in the harbor. The English fleet could not get close enough to let their soldiers land. They decided to bomb Fort McHenry. Cannons went off all day and all night. Peoples' homes shook from top to bottom. No shots were fired from Fort McHenry. The guns at the fort could not shoot far enough to reach the ships in the harbor. After midnight a party of English *barges* slipped toward shore. They intended to land their troops. A guard at Fort McHenry heard them and sounded the alarm. Guns from the fort and the city fired on the English, who retreated to their ships.

Francis Scott Key was a Maryland lawyer. Dr. William Beanes of Upper Marlboro had been captured by the British. Before the battle started, Key went to the British fleet. He tried to get Dr. Beanes freed. The English accepted his plan, but Key and Beanes had to stay on the English ship until the battle was over. The next morning they saw the flag flying over Fort McHenry. They knew the Americans had won. Key later wrote a poem. The poem became "The Star Spangled Banner," our *national anthem.*

THE STORY OF OUR NATIONAL ANTHEM

Dear Diary

Today was a wonderful day. Mr. Key and Dr. Beanes returned after being held by the English during the Battle of Baltimore. Everyone was afraid we would never see Dr. Beanes again. General Ross was staying at Dr. Beanes's house when the English marched through our town on their way to Washington, D.C.

When the soldiers arrived in Washington, they burned our new capital city. Most of the English soldiers marched back to their ships. Some soldiers did bad things. They stole from people at gunpoint.

When Dr. Beanes heard about what happened, he and two other men arrested the soldiers. One English soldier who saw this told General Ross. The general sent soldiers back to Dr. Beanes's house. They got Dr. Beanes and the other two men and put them in jail. The next morning, we found out Dr. Beanes had been thrown into the jail on board ship. The ship then sailed to Baltimore.

Mr. Francis Scott Key, a well-known and trusted lawyer, was asked to help. Mr. Key got permission from President Madison to go to Baltimore and arrange for Dr. Beanes's release. Mr. Key won Dr. Beanes's freedom, but they had to stay on board the ship in the harbor. Both men heard the English planning what they were going to do in the battle. Mr. Key walked back and forth on the deck all night. He was worried that the English would win the battle.

Baltimore and Ft. McHenry were ready for the English. They fought them all night. There was so much noise. The cannons were booming and people were yelling. Mr. Key wrote down things as they happened.

When the sun came up the next morning, September 14, they could see the huge flag. It was 36 feet long, 29 feet wide, and it was still flying. That made them cheer. The English had to give up the fight.

Tonight we found out what Mr. Key was writing during the battle. It was a very beautiful poem, and the words fit a tune we know.

Goodnight diary, until tomorrow.
Emily Brooke Andrews

FRANCIS SCOTT KEY, 1779-1843

Francis Scott Key's family came to America from England in the 1700s. His father fought in the Revolutionary War. During his childhood, Francis Scott Key lived with his parents on their plantation near Frederick. When he entered St. John's College in Annapolis, he lived with his great-aunt.

While he studied law he also worked for his uncle Philip Key, a lawyer, and Judge Samuel Chase. He met Mary Lloyd in Annapolis. When he finished his studies he married her in the Lloyd home. It was one of the fanciest weddings of the time. They made their home in Georgetown, where their children were born.

All during his life, Francis Scott Key loved to write. He wrote poems.

If Dr. William Beanes of Upper Marlboro had not been held on the British war ship, Francis Scott Key would not have seen the bombardment. Do you suppose he would have written his famous poem anyway?

He sometimes even wrote notes to his wife during dinner about their guests. Key was a very religious person and had often said he would like to be a minister. He wrote two hymns and helped found a school to train ministers.

Key was a very good friend of President Andrew Jackson. President Jackson selected Key to be the district attorney for Washington, D.C.

Key was sent to Alabama to settle a dispute between the Creek Indians and the settlers. Several people had been killed before he arrived. He won the trust of the citizens through his poetry and gentle ways. A peaceful settlement was reached. The Creek Indian Reservation was created without further bloodshed.

Key is also remembered for his work to return slaves to Africa. Later he worked for their freedom.

The Last Battle

The English gathered their men and left Baltimore and Chesapeake Bay. The last battle of the War of 1812 was fought in New Orleans, Louisiana. The battle was fought fifteen days after the peace treaty was signed between the United States and England. This was because communication was poor. General Andrew Jackson was in charge of the troops. Jackson would later become one of our presidents. He had a strong, well-disciplined army. The English were badly defeated. England lost another great general and 2,000 English soldiers in this battle. It was a battle that never should have started.

Peace was reached in 1815. The United States won respect all over the world. The dwarf fought the giant and remained free. Washington, D.C., was rebuilt and grew in beauty.

This very new nation had made many mistakes in the War of 1812. Now it was over. The country was stronger and very proud. The people turned their attention to developing the many resources of the land. They now paid more attention to their own country than to Europe. It remained this way for the next 100 years.

WORDS TO KNOW

STUDY

barge

blockade

fell

flotilla

hymn

maneuver

national anthem

run the blockade

QUESTIONS TO ANSWER

1. What two countries started the War of 1812?

2. What measure did England and France use to keep each other from receiving supplies?

3. On which country did the United States Congress declare war?

4. How did the town of St. Michael's fool the English navy?

5. What navy officer led a flotilla of gunboats in a battle in the Patuxent River?

6. What were the "Bladensburg Races"?

7. What was General Strickler's task in helping to defend Baltimore?

8. When did Francis Scott Key write "The Star Spangled Banner"?

9. Where was the last battle of the War of 1812 fought?

INTERPRETING WHAT YOU HAVE READ

10. Explain how better communications might have saved lives in 1815 in New Orleans.

11. "The dwarf fought the giant and remained free." What does that mean?

THINGS TO DISCUSS

12. How was the War of 1812 different from a war our country might have today?

View of Lower Jones Falls. The painting is by Francis Guy.

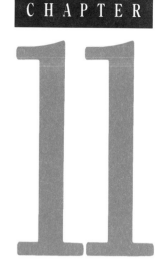

A New Economy, 1818-1860

What is Economy?

Economy is the way goods and services are spread out and used among the people. It is the way they make a living. A state's economy is described by its farm and factory products, its service businesses, and the wealth these businesses make.

The economy of Maryland had started to change before the Revolutionary War. Grain replaced tobacco as the major crop. Annapolis remained the state's capital, but it was no longer a busy port. Baltimore had become the center of business in Maryland.

Baltimore, Commercial Center

There were several reasons why Baltimore became the state's *commercial* (kuh-MER-shul) center. The city was blessed with natural ways to make power. Jones Falls meant there could be water power. The land around Baltimore also made it easy to connect with western Maryland and southern Pennsylvania.

The government built a *customs* house in Baltimore in 1790. This is a place where goods entering the United States are checked. The items must match a list given to the customs inspector. Taxes have to be paid on these goods. People saw that Baltimore was now the state's commercial center.

The main harbor in Baltimore, however, was filling with *sediment* from Jones Falls and Herring Run. Fells Point then became important for shipping goods to other states.

New Roads Needed

In the late 1700s the people, the state, and the tiny country grew in many ways.

The people pushing west from Maryland settled and built homes in the Ohio River Valley. They raised cattle and grain. It was hard for them to get their products to market because of the roads. There was already a good road running between Baltimore and Cumberland. Now a road was needed from the Ohio Valley to Cumberland and on to the coast.

National Road

The Congress and president had good news for Marylanders. The national government decided to pay for this road since it would run through several states. It would be called the National Road. It was agreed that the road would start in

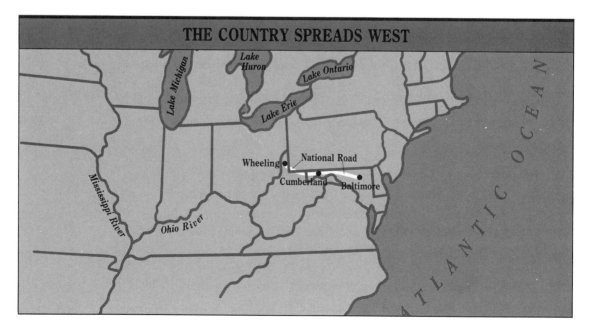

THE COUNTRY SPREADS WEST

La Vale Toll Gate House in Allegany County. This is the first toll gate on the National Road in Maryland. It is a seven-sided building. It is one of only two toll houses built on the road in Maryland.

Cumberland. It would go to the western farm lands. This meant the National Road would lead straight to Baltimore. Merchants and shippers of Baltimore were very happy with this news.

Such a road had been the dream of George Washington. He had been over the mountains and knew the land was *fertile*. He felt that people would live there someday. However, he died before it happened. President Thomas Jefferson had the road laid out in 1806. By 1818 the 130 miles of road between Cumberland and Wheeling, Virginia, were open. (Wheeling later became part of West Virginia.)

The National Road was built with great care. It was 30 feet wide. There were 25-foot strips cleared of trees and brush on each side of the road. The road had to cross several mountains, the highest being 2,328 feet above sea level. It took a lot of work to cut down the steep hills. The roadbed had to be graded, or smoothed out. A layer of broken stones one foot thick covered the road. Another layer of smaller stones was put on top of that. Can you guess some possible reasons for this? The center of the road was slightly higher

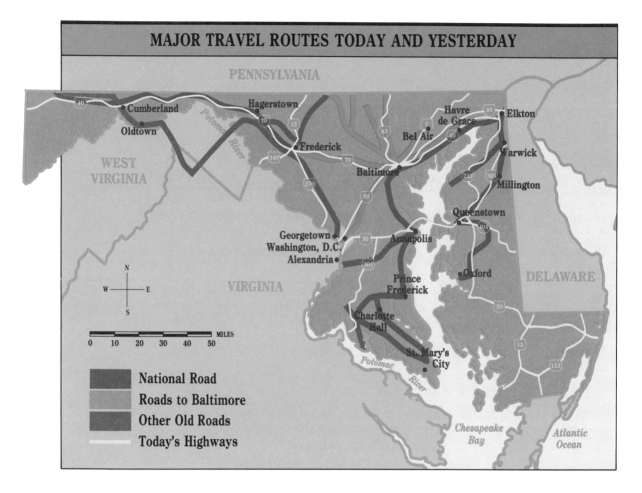

MAJOR TRAVEL ROUTES TODAY AND YESTERDAY

National Road

Roads to Baltimore

Other Old Roads

Today's Highways

than its edges. This allowed water and snow to drain off the road into the ditches on both sides.

When the *toll* road opened, a flood of traffic was ready. Conestoga wagons (covered wagons) carried large loads of tobacco, grain, whisky, furs, and other goods. Stagecoaches carried people to and from different cities. Herds of cattle, pigs, and sheep were driven to market over this great road. The road was what George Washington had wanted. It brought the East and West together.

Life on the National Road was exciting. Stagecoaches brought letters and newspapers to towns. The letters and papers were read eagerly. Many people found work along the highway. Some became wagon drivers. Some opened shops which built carriages, made whips, or fashioned and repaired wheels. Stonemasons (men who build with stone) built bridges. Some worked at repairing the road. Other men worked as tollhouse keepers. These people lived in certain houses along the road and collected the tolls.

People who depended on the road for their work were known as "pike boys." It didn't matter how old or how young they were. They were still called pike boys. Can you figure out why?

In 1852 the Baltimore and Ohio Railroad reached Wheeling from Baltimore. It was a faster and cheaper way to carry goods and people. In a short time fewer wagons and coaches were using the road.

Much of today's Route 40 follows the path of the old National Road. An old tollhouse still stands on Route 40 near Cumberland.

Building a Canal

It was a dream of many people to use the Potomac River to go further west. The Chesapeake and Ohio Canal was planned to connect Washington, D.C., and Cumberland. Finally it was started in 1828. John Quincy Adams, president of the United

This painting from the C & O Canal Museum shows workmen digging the canal bed. Many of the workers were Irishmen.

States, broke ground for this waterway.

Many men were hired to do many different kinds of work. Immigrants from Ireland and Holland found jobs here. Some felled trees. Others rode horses that pulled scrapers to move earth. Still others used picks and shovels to haul away the dirt in wheelbarrows and wagons. Stonemasons built big gates called *locks*. The locks would lift the boats 605 feet between Georgetown and Cumberland. The canal company hoped to make money by charging a toll.

The workmen lived in camps while the canal was being built. Living conditions were poor. Many workers became sick. Often the canal company did not have money to pay the workers. The workers would sometimes *riot* when this happened.

Aqueduct at Williamsport, in Washington County. The canal crossed the Conococheague Creek through an aqueduct, or bridge built to carry water. You can see the mules towing a boat along the canal.

Life on the C & O Canal

After many years of hard work and problems, the waterway reached Cumberland in 1850. It was 185 miles long. There were 74 locks on it.

The flat-bottomed canal boats were about 92 feet long and 14 feet wide. They could carry 120 tons of cargo. There were small cabins at the *stern* (back) of the boats. The cabins held several bunk beds. There was also a small kitchen on board. A stable for mules was at the boat's *bow* (front). A hay house for the mules was in the middle.

Mules were important on the canal. A mule walked along a towpath attached to a rope tied to the front of the boat. In this way the mules pulled the boats up and down the canal. While one mule walked, another rested. A mule's work shift was about six hours long. Then came a rest. The mules were treated well by the mule drivers, who were known as a "hoggees" (hog-EEZ).

The families of canal boat captains lived on the boats. Can you think of good points about living on the canal? What might be hard about that way of life?

The boats carried flour, grain, building stone, and coal from Cumberland to Georgetown. The trip took five or six days. The boat from Georgetown to Cumberland took less time because it carried a lighter load of fish, fertilizer, salt, iron ore, and store goods. By the 1870s, 500 boats making many trips were carrying about 250,000 tons of cargo a year.

The Chesapeake and Ohio Canal did not make money for the merchants. It was in *debt* (DET) from the beginning. It also was *competing* against the railroad. The waterway was finally closed to business in 1924 after a heavy flood badly damaged it.

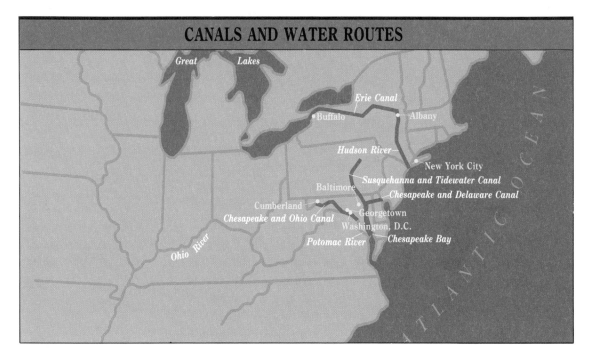

CANALS AND WATER ROUTES

Other Canals

Maryland merchants tried to move their goods with another canal in 1803. It was known as the Susquehanna and Tidewater Canal. It also failed.

The Chesapeake and Delaware Canal, opened in 1829, was successful. In fact, it is still used today. It links Delaware Bay with the Chesapeake Bay. Ships use this canal because it saves them many miles on their way from Baltimore to Philadelphia. Ocean-going ships also use it on their way from Baltimore to ports on the North Atlantic and in Europe. The C & D Canal is very important to the Port of Baltimore.

In 1825 states around the Great Lakes began moving goods to New York City over the Erie Canal in New York. Pennsylvania was also making plans to get more business. Baltimore wanted its share of the Great Lakes trade. Its connections with the Ohio River Valley had to be improved.

Baltimore and Ohio Railroad

Baltimore bankers and merchants planned a railroad. It was named the Baltimore and Ohio. A big celebration was held when the first stone of the railroad was laid. Officers of the railroad, soldiers of the nation's wars, and important guests rode in fancy carriages. Farmers, millers, bankers, and other workers from 50 trades followed on wagons. Charles Carroll of Carrollton stepped forward. He was the only signer of the Declaration of Independence who was still living. He turned the first shovelful of earth to start the railroad company. This act meant a great deal to the people. Charles Carroll was greatly loved by the people. His taking part seemed to mean that all would go well.

The United States already had a few railroads. Most did not have many miles of rail. Few people knew anything about running a railroad, especially one that would carry people as well as goods.

What Kind of Engine?

There were many questions to be asked. The biggest question was how to power the train's engine. Wind power using sails had been tried without luck. It upset the car and the passengers were thrown into a ditch. Another way was to have a horse walk on a *treadmill.* That didn't work either. The car bumped into a cow and went off the track.

A New York merchant named Peter Cooper proved that a steam engine would work. His engine was called the *Tom Thumb.* The *Tom Thumb* pulled a train to Ellicott Mills, thirteen miles west of Baltimore, and back. It could go ten to twelve miles an hour. By 1832 there were other engines drawing loaded railroad cars.

Tom Thumb, *the first locomotive built in America. In this picture, the* Tom Thumb *is part of a parade in 1927.*

Railroad Business Booms

By 1830 passengers were making short trips. Flour was sent to Baltimore from Ellicott Mills. By 1835 a line linked Baltimore with Washington, D.C. In 1842 the B & O ran to Cumberland. In 1852 it reached Wheeling, Virginia, and the Ohio River.

There was a steady flow of goods and passengers as far as the line went. It was making money. Raw materials and manufactured goods began to be shipped from Wheeling to Baltimore. The city got its share of the western trade. As factories, mills, and shops in Baltimore grew, people gained wealth. Ships also crowded the city's harbor.

In 1827 bankers and merchants decided to build a railroad to the West Coast (California). It was called the transcontinental railroad and was finished in 1869. It completely united the

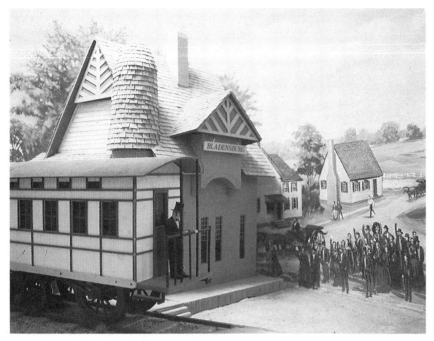

In 1851 Charles Grafton Page finished the first run of his battery-powered locomotive. Onlookers were surprised when it pull into Bladensburg. It had no smoke or puffing of steam. It was quieter than any train they had heard before.

country. This was a great service to all the American people. Improved means of transportation helped the country's businesses to grow. Products were also being shipped to Europe. Trade was never better.

Steam Engine for Ships

Now came the time for a change in transportation on the water. The clipper ships of the Chesapeake Bay had to give way to the giant steamships.

James Rumsey, who had lived during George Washington's time, had kept a secret. One day he invited Washington to see his new boat in Berkeley Springs, Virginia. Rumsey started his boat near Harper's Ferry with six passengers aboard. The boat moved by steam up the Potomac. Its engine pulled water in through the front of the boat and forced it out behind. This made the boat go forward even against the current. Rumsey died before he could build a bigger boat. Two men, however, picked up on his idea. They built steamboats using some of Rumsey's ideas.

It wasn't long before steamboats were traveling every-

View of Baltimore, 1847. Can you find the steamboats in the painting?

where. Baltimore lost some of its shipping power, but goods still came to the city over the railroad lines. The Atlantic coast cities were in a race to see which could get the most trade. Baltimore became the second greatest port shipping goods to other countries around the world.

Industrial Revolution

In the early 1800s Maryland was part of the Industrial Revolution. During this time machinery began to take the place of people who worked with their hands. Instead of a person spinning cotton by hand, a machine could do it faster. Inventions such as the sewing machine improved the clothing business. There were many other machines that made people's work faster and easier.

New reapers could cut many fields of grain in a short time. The refrigerator kept food fresh. People could send messages across miles of space with Morse's telegraph.

Rembrandt Peale, who opened a museum, announced he would light the building with a new kind of light. It was a gas light made from coal. People liked it so much that the Baltimore city council decided to use gas lights in the streets. Baltimore became the third city in the world to use gas lights.

As new inventions were accepted, people changed their ways of living. What seemed impossible one day became real the next.

Businesses became larger. The small shop that had one or two workers was being replaced by a factory. Owning a factory was a new way to become rich.

This happy time of progress would soon be slowed down. The coming Civil War would upset everyone's way of life. It would also tear the country apart.

Cyrus McCormick's reaper gets its first test in 1831.

STUDY

WORDS TO KNOW

bow (on a boat)   lock
commercial   riot
compete   sediment
customs   stern
economy   toll
debt   treadmill
fertile

QUESTIONS TO ANSWER

1. What makes up a state's economy?
2. What replaced tobacco as the major crop before the Revolutionary War?
3. What city became Maryland's commercial center?
4. What road was built between Cumberland, Maryland, and Wheeling, Virginia?
5. What new travel route was easier and faster than the National Road?
6. Name the water route that connected Cumberland and Washington, D.C.

7. Name four things that were hauled from Cumberland to Georgetown on the C & O Canal.

8. Who decided to build the Baltimore and Ohio Railroad?

9. What kind of power replaced sails for moving ships in the water?

10. What is another name for the early 1800s, when machines began to replace people who had worked with their hands?

INTERPRETING WHAT YOU HAVE READ

11. How did the National Road get its name?

12. Why did most of the canals go out of business?

THINGS TO DISCUSS

13. Suppose you are traveling from Georgetown to Cumberland in 1835. What kind of transportation would you choose? Give your reasons. How long would the trip take? How much time would the trip take using today's transportation?

Black slaves were thought to be an important part of the plantation economy. These workers are weeding a field of young tobacco plants.

CHAPTER

Civil War, 1860-1865

Why the War Started

The Civil War was a great turning point in United States history. It was fought between citizens of the United States.

There were several causes of the war. One was the slavery *issue*. The states in the South were in favor of slavery. Those in the north were against slavery. Northern states passed laws saying people could not hold slaves who were runaways. Runaway slaves who went to these states were treated as free people. The South was angry about this. *Secession* (seh-SEH-shun) was another reason for the war. The South believed any state could secede, or leave, the Union. The North did not agree with that, nor did the United States government.

At this time in history (1860s), there were three very large geographic parts of the United States. They were the Northeast, the West, and the South. The Northeast included all of the New England states, Pennsylvania, New York, and New Jersey. The states of Ohio to the Minnesota Territory were called the West. The South was the states from Maryland to Texas.

CIVIL WAR STATES

Union (North)
Confederacy (South)
Unsettled

Economy of the States

Each part of the country had different ways of making money. Most people in the South were farmers. They grew such things as cotton, tobacco, and sugar cane. They exported these crops to Europe. People in the West also farmed. Their crops were mostly grain. They sold these goods to the northeastern states. The Northeast, in turn, sent the West manufactured (man-uh-FAK-cherd) goods.

People in the northeastern and western states got along well. They shared a similar way of life. Both the Northeast and the West had large cities. They had large populations. They did not believe in owning slaves.

Many people in the South lived on large plantations. There were few cities in the South. Those states needed many people to do the work of raising cotton. Southerners believed that slaves were the key to raising huge crops.

Underground Railroad

Abolitionists started the Underground Railroad to help free slaves. This wasn't a railroad at all. It was made up of houses or other places where slaves were hidden during the day. Many times slaves were hidden in a dark cellar. They might also be hidden in a swamp. During the night, the slaves were guided north toward freedom.

A book called *Uncle Tom's Cabin* was written about slave life. Harriet Beecher Stowe was the author. Her book told of the hardships slaves faced. It helped many people understand that slavery was cruel. More people in the North were then willing to help slaves escape. But the book made Southerners angry.

This etching shows slaves leaving their homes to escape on the Underground Railroad. How do you think these people felt?

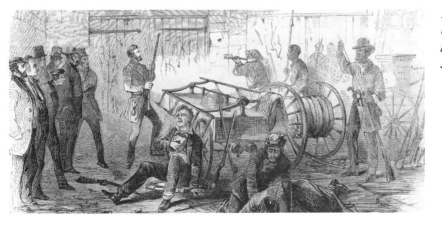

Inside the fire engine house just before the gate is broken down by John Brown's group.

John Brown's Raid

An abolitionist named John Brown led a raid on Harper's Ferry in Virginia. This was where guns and gunpowder were made and stored. Brown hoped to take over the *arsenal* (AR-sun-ul) and then start a slave *uprising*. His plan failed. He was caught and later hanged.

The South felt the abolitionists were a real danger. They thought the Northern leaders had encouraged John Brown. They also blamed the North for the fact that their slaves were running away.

Abraham Lincoln was elected president in 1860. He wanted to end slavery. He also favored other things the South was against. He did not want any states to withdraw from the Union.

Southern States Secede

South Carolina seceded in December 1860. It was the first state to leave the Union. By March 1861 Mississippi, Florida, Alabama, Georgia, Louisiana, and Texas had also withdrawn.

In February of that year, representatives from these states met in Montgomery, Alabama. There they joined together as the Confederate States of America. Jefferson Davis became their president.

Attack on Fort Sumter

President Lincoln said that secession was against the law. He warned the states that he would hold onto any land and buildings in the South. Lincoln sent supplies to Fort Sumter in April 1861. Fort Sumter was in South Carolina, which had not left the Union.

The South then attacked Fort Sumter. The fort surrendered after 33 hours of being shelled. President Lincoln called for soldiers to uphold the country's laws. The South said this was the same as declaring war. Virginia, Arkansas, North Carolina, and Tennessee joined the Confederacy.

The South was very happy to get Virginia. This state had a large population and waterfront on the Chesapeake Bay.

Inside Fort Sumter during the bombardment.

Richmond became the capitol of the Confederacy.

Robert E. Lee was offered *field command* of the Union. He did not want a war. He felt he could not fight against his home state, Virginia. He would be fighting his own family if this happened. He quit the Union army. He then became an advisor to the Confederate (Southern) president. Lee was made a general in the Confederate army in May 1861. He commanded the Army of Northern Virginia.

Maryland's Place in the War

Maryland was a border state. It sat between the Northern and Southern states. When Fort Sumter surrendered, Marylanders were divided in their feelings. People in the western and northern parts of the state favored the North. Southern Marylanders and some Eastern Shore people favored the South. Many people in Baltimore also wanted to fight on the side of the South.

Anna Ella Carroll, a woman from Maryland, warned President Lincoln that certain legislators would try to have Maryland fight on the side of the South. He quickly had those men arrested. They were sent to prisons in the North. President Lincoln placed Union soldiers in Baltimore and other important cities of Maryland. The soldiers could search any home where they suspected people were helping the South. Maryland stayed in the Union because of pressure from President Lincoln. Not all Marylanders, though, were pleased with this action.

Maryland in the Middle

In April 1861 the first blood of the Civil War was shed in Maryland. It happened on Pratt Street in Baltimore during what is known as the Baltimore Riot. A group of people who favored the South attacked some Union soldiers. The soldiers were on their way to Washington, D.C. They were trying to move from one train station to another. Some citizens yelled insults and threw rocks at the soldiers. Many soldiers were hurt. Finally, a shot rang out. One soldier fell dead. The soldiers then turned and fired into the crowd. Several people were killed. Police formed a line between the soldiers and the crowd. This allowed the soldiers to hurry back to the train station.

Artist's view of the massacre at Baltimore. Several people were killed.

A LETTER TO A COUSIN

Baltimore

19 April 1861

Dear Cousin,

I must tell you what I saw today. I am afraid we are going to be in a war. This may be my last letter to you for awhile. People say we will be fighting our relatives. I'll never fight you, Joseph.

I was walking on Pratt Street to

meet Father. As I walked, I could hear all kinds of yelling. I couldn't see what was happening. I pushed through a group of people and saw soldiers being struck with stones and clubs.

You would have been as scared as I was. People were yelling "traitor" and "kill them!" I couldn't move. I was frozen in my spot. I was pushed back and forth by these angry people.

All at once I heard a man holler something. Then there was a loud crack and a puff of smoke. A soldier fell on the street. He was bleeding. Before I could even look up, the soldiers shot their guns. Several people fell down. A man near me screamed and grabbed his arm. When I saw the blood, I got sick to my stomach.

All of a sudden someone snatched me by the arm. My feet were flying. We ran a long time before we finally stopped. I looked up to see my father. He was crying, Joseph. I've never seen my father cry before. He didn't say a word. He didn't have to.

Later today we found out four soldiers were killed. One must have been the poor man I saw. I'm glad Father got me out of there. I don't think I could have moved otherwise. My legs felt like they were iron.

Joseph, I hope we won't go to war. Please write back and tell me what is happening in North Carolina. Do you live near Fort Sumter? I shall wait patiently for your reply.

Your cousin,
David Goldfarble

Word of the riot reached Marylander James Ryder Randall. He was teaching school in Louisiana at the time. Randall believed in the cause of the South. His heart was touched when he heard about the fight. He was so moved that he wrote a poem called "My Maryland." The words of the poem were put to music. "Maryland, My Maryland" was a favorite song of men serving in the Confederate army. In 1939 it became the official state song. Some different words were later written but have not been approved by the state legislature.

The United States government made a big decision in 1861. The Naval Academy was moved from Annapolis to Newport, Rhode Island. There was a feeling in Maryland that the Confederacy might capture Annapolis. Moving the students of

James Ryder Randall wrote a poem that later became the Maryland state song.

the Naval Academy further north kept them safe. They were moved back to Annapolis after the Civil War.

The First Battle

From the beginning of the war, the Union believed they had the *advantage*. They thought they would defeat the Confederates. People from Washington came out to watch the first battle. They even brought picnic lunches. The battle was held in Manassas, Virginia. It was called the Battle of Bull Run. The Union army did poorly in this battle. The roads were soon filled with picnickers and soldiers hurrying back to Washington. It was during this battle that General "Stonewall" Jackson of the South got his nickname. He would not allow his men to panic. He stayed in the thick of battle and kept order.

Cutting Off the South from the West

Again Anna Ella Carroll came up with a good plan. It was to capture Fort Henry and Fort Donelson in Tennessee. The forts were strong on the river side. Carroll said they were weak on the land side. A. H. Foate was to lead an attack from the river. Ulysses S. Grant was to come in from behind by land.

Lincoln liked the plan. The battle was carried out success-fully. Through Carroll's plan, the South was cut off from the West. The South's main railroad was in the Union's hands.

All this time, the South hoped England would help them fight the North. Those hopes were dimmed after Admiral David G. Farragut led a Union attack on New Orleans. He captured the city and placed a blockade off the Louisiana coast. The South knew England would not enter the war now. The South was alone in the fight.

Iron Ships Used in Battle

Another battle was fought in March 1862. It was a naval battle. This was the first time iron ships were used in war.

The South had built a ship made of iron. It was called the *Merrimack*. The *Merrimack* steamed into Hampton Roads, Virginia, which was in Union hands. The Merrimack fired on the wooden ships anchored there. The wooden ships were blasted to pieces. Then a Union ship called the *Monitor* appeared. It was also made of iron. It had just barely been finished. The two ships fought. The *Merrimack* was forced back into the Norfolk harbor. It never came out again. Union forces captured the *Merrimack* before it was repaired. Clearly, the day of wooden ships was over.

Grant Leads Troops into Maryland

In the West, General Grant moved up the Tennessee River.

Artist's view of the battle of the Monitor *and* Merrimac.

He hoped to cut off all supplies to the South. Grant moved to a place called Shiloh. A terrible battle took place there. Each side lost about 1,700 men, and thousands were wounded. Hundreds were listed as missing. The battle was fought April 6 and 7, 1862. Grant gained a victory, pushing the Southern troops back.

General Lee moved his men into Maryland in September 1862. Some of the men with him were Marylanders. They were so happy to be back in Maryland they fell down on their knees and kissed the soil. Their clothing was torn and ragged. Some didn't even have shoes.

The Confederates marched into Frederick, Maryland. General Lee asked Maryland men to join his army. He did not get many men to help him. The people in Frederick favored the Union.

BARBARA FRITCHIE

During the Civil War, General Thomas "Stonewall" Jackson crossed into Maryland. He camped outside the town of Frederick. Barbara Fritchie had called this town her home for 93 years. She loved her country and was very loyal to the Union cause.

Jackson and his men stayed in Frederick four days. They hoped to get the men from the town to join their side. This did not happen.

On the fifth day, the Confederates broke camp. They marched through the towns right past Fritchie's home. There are several stories of what happened that day, but the most likely story follows.

Fritchie was told the troops were coming. She thought they would be Union troops. She hurried to the window waving the Union flag. A Confederate soldier saw this and warned her to take the flag inside.

Fritchie realized then the soldiers were Confederates. However, she refused to move and kept waving the flag. The soldier called to his officer, asking for permission to shoot Fritchie.

John Greenleaf Whittier wrote a poem about Fritchie. This is how he says the story ended:

"Shoot if you must, this old gray head,
But spare your country's flag," she said.
A shade of sadness, a blush of shame,
Over the face of the leader came.
The nobler nature within him stirred
To life at that woman's deed and word,
"Who touches a hair of yon gray head
Dies like a dog! March on!" he said.

A stone tablet marks the place where this event took place. Barbara Fritchie's home in Frederick is open to visitors.

Talk about these questions with members of your class:

1. How did Barbara Fritchie feel about the Union?

2. How did the Confederate leader feel after Fritchie took her stand? What did he do to show how he felt?

3. "The nobler nature within him stirred to life." What does this mean?

Battle of Antietam Creek

Union General George McClellan met General Lee's Confederates eight days later. They fought at South Mountain. The Confederates had to move back near Sharpsburg. They were greatly outnumbered. For two days the armies fought fiercely. Neither side really won. Lee's army was so weakened that he moved his men back to Virginia.

This battle is known as the Battle of Antietam Creek. Sometimes it is called the Battle of Sharpsburg. It was fought on September 18, 1862. It was one of the worst battles of the Civil War. More than 25,000 men were killed or badly wounded.

Battle of Antietam,
*September 17, 1862,
at Burnside's Bridge.*

*This is a street in
Sharpsburg about the
time of the Battle of
Antietam. Every avail-
able building was
being used for shelter
or to care for the
wounded.*

Battles were being fought in other parts of the South and as far west as Mississippi.

While Ulysses S. Grant was in Mississippi, Lee crossed into Maryland again. He was going to Pennsylvania. He also wanted to capture either Philadelphia or Baltimore on his way. General George G. Meade was sent after Lee.

Battle of Gettysburg

General Lee raided southern Pennsylvania and then moved his
men southwest. There, at a town called Gettysburg, the two
armies met. In a three-day battle, Lee was defeated. The Battle of Gettysburg is perhaps the best-known battle in United
States history. It took place in July 1863.

Lee retreated into Virginia. Losses were heavy on both
sides. There were no hospitals. The wounded could be given
very little help. In time, the dead were buried.

A memorial service was held and President Lincoln gave a
speech. This speech, known as the Gettysburg Address, is
famous.

Defending Maryland

In Maryland, General Jubal Early of the South was fighting
near Frederick and Washington, D.C. General Lew Wallace of
the North tried to stop Early. Early won in Frederick. The
battle, however, gave the Union time to build up power in
Washington, D.C. Early was defeated there and moved back
to Virginia.

Many other small battles were fought in Maryland. Sometimes the Confederates captured towns and took money and
food from the people.

General Jubal Early led his army into Maryland in 1864.
Early stayed in Hagerstown and Frederick. He forced the
people to pay him large sums of money. If they hadn't paid,
their towns would have been burned. These cities have asked
Congress several times to repay them for their losses.

The War Ends

After a chain of battles, General Lee at last gave in to General
Grant. He surrendered at Appomatox Courthouse, Virginia.

The South was fully *ravaged*. Plantations had been
burned. Businesses were smashed. Railways and cities were
in ruin. Families sobbed for their loved ones.

Soldiers on both sides returned home. Many men held in
prison camps were sick or dying. Prisoners on both sides had
been treated *disgracefully*. Men were allowed to starve and

suffer from cold and sickness. They lived in filthy places filled with *vermin*. Some of the prisons in Maryland were Fort McHenry and Point Lookout in St. Mary's County. There is a state park, museum, and Confederate cemetery at Point Lookout.

The war was over. The slaves were free. The country was no longer divided. It would still take many years for people on both sides to forgive.

This cartoon was drawn by a prisoner held at Point Lookout during the Civil War. The people in the picture are making fun of the man who had never seen a crab before.

Lincoln Assassinated

Another tragic thing happened on April 14, 1865. President Lincoln was killed. He was shot by John Wilkes Booth. Booth felt President Lincoln caused the Civil War. As Lincoln watched a play in Ford's Theater, Booth shot him in the head. Booth then leaped from the president's box, where Lincoln was sitting, to the stage. He broke his leg in the fall. Booth rode on horseback to Charles County where Dr. Samuel Mudd set his broken leg. From there he crossed the Potomac River to Virginia.

Booth planned the *assassination* (uh-sas-uh-NAY-shun) with several people. Booth and his companion, David E. Herold, were trapped in a barn. The barn was set on fire to force the men out. Herold gave himself up, but Booth was killed.

Mary Surratt's inn. John Wilkes Booth and one of his partners stopped here on the way to Ford's Theater in Washington, D.C. At the inn they picked up guns and supplies that were hidden there. Mary Surratt was hanged for her part in the plan. This picture is from a diorama.

Booth's partners in the plot were tried by a jury. Four went to jail and four were hanged. Mary Surratt of Maryland was one of the four people hanged. The group had planned to kill President Lincoln in her boarding house.

It would have been better for the South had Booth failed in his plan. President Lincoln planned to get the South back into the Union with the least possible *harshness*. He also planned to educate the slaves. He wanted them to enter into a free life able to take care of themselves. As it turned out, the South was treated harshly. Free blacks had a hard time making a living for themselves.

Marylanders Help the South Rebuild

Maryland was ruled by the military throughout the war. Soldiers finally withdrew in 1866.

It was also in 1866 that a great fair was held in Baltimore. The South needed a great deal of money and help to rebuild. A group of Baltimore women formed the Southern Relief Association. Through the fair, $160,000 was raised, and the Maryland state government gave $100,000 more. George Peabody, a Marylander, gave $2,000,000. This money was sent to the South. It was to build and pay for upkeep on a school. With this helping hand, and much more work, the South was able to make a new start.

Maryland Gets Back to Business

At the beginning of the Civil War, ships were not allowed to leave Baltimore. The Union was afraid people would ship food or weapons to the South. This hurt business in Maryland. The law was lifted, however, before the war was over. New businesses came to the city. Supplies from the North came for the Union soldiers in Maryland. Marylanders found a market for their crops in the Northern States. Maryland's trade and factory businesses grew because of its location. In many ways, it was helpful to be a border state.

After the war, many white Southerners came to Baltimore. They could not find work in the South. Many freed blacks also came to Maryland. The state moved ahead in wealth and numbers of people.

STUDY

WORDS TO KNOW

advantage	issue
arsenal	ravaged
assassination	secession
disgracefully	uprising
field command	vermin
harsh	

QUESTIONS TO ANSWER

1. Who fought the Civil War?
2. What were two causes of the Civil War?
3. Name the three large geographic parts of the United States in 1860. To which part did Maryland belong?
4. What book helped people understand the cruelty of slavery?

5. Who was president of the Confederate States of America?
6. Control of what fort later led to the start of the Civil War?
7. Who was offered a job as a Union army officer, but decided to join the Confederacy instead?
8. Where was the first blood shed in Maryland?
9. What is Maryland's official state song? Who wrote the words?
10. Name the first battle of the Civil War.
11. What kind of ships were used in war for the first time in 1862?
12. What did Barbara Fritchie do that made the Confederate army angry?
13. Who was the commander of the Union Army to whom General Lee surrendered?
14. When and where did the Civil War end?
15. What happened to President Lincoln in April 1865?

INTERPRETING WHAT YOU HAVE READ

16. What leading product did each of the three parts of the United States produce in 1860?
17. Why did Maryland remain a Union state even though many Marylanders fought for the Confederacy?
18. In which part of Maryland were Civil War battles fought?
19. Why was John Brown considered dangerous by both the North and the South?

THINGS TO DISCUSS

20. How did Baltimore help the South recover after the war? Does this kind of thing happen today? Give some examples.

A bird's-eye view of Baltimore in 1858. By then it had become crowded with houses and other buildings.

Booming Baltimore, 1865-1910

13

America Spreads West

A fter the Civil War the population of the United States was growing very fast. Europeans were coming to America by the thousands. The people were spreading west where the land was cheap. The center of the country was now in Indiana.

Baltimore Becomes a Major Population Center

Maryland, like the rest of the country, was growing. In the 1880s the number of people in the Old Line State grew to one million.

One-third of the people in Baltimore were immigrants or the children of immigrants. Baltimore was the largest city in Maryland and became much larger from 1870 to 1900. By 1900 there were over a half million people living there. The number of blacks in the city grew quickly. Immigrants from Europe came by the thousands through Locust Point.

After Baltimore, the next largest cities in population were Cumberland, Hagerstown, and Annapolis. Each had a little more than 10,000 people.

Up until 1900 Maryland had been a farm state. This began to change. Manufacturing, trade, mining, and transporta-

These immigrants at Locust Point are probably from Poland. What do you think they have in the bags and trunks?

tion became the state's important industries.

Most of the land was still farm land, but most of the people lived in the cities. By 1900 half of all the people living in Maryland lived in one city—Baltimore.

Railroads Improved

The railroads had been used for hauling supplies during the Civil War. The railroads were valuable. Large amounts of goods could be moved quickly on trains.

In the early 1900s, Baltimore businessmen built up the railroads even more. The Atlantic Coast Line and Seaboard Air Line ran to the South. Baltimore became known as the Gateway to the South.

JOHN W. GARRETT, RAILROAD MAN

Johh W. Garrett was a very important railroad developer. *He became president of the Baltimore and Ohio Railroad in 1858. At that time the railroad was not making money. Within two years, Garrett turned the railroad business around. He didn't add many miles of track, but he made sure the line was repaired and in good order.*

During the Civil War, Garrett arranged for a special train to take President Abraham Lincoln to the Antietam battlefield. The B & O Railroad was very important to the Union Army. It helped move soldiers quickly.

After the Civil War, Garrett added many miles of track and many stations to the railroad line. The B & O connected the Delaware River and the Chesapeake Bay on the east with the Mississippi River and the Great Lakes to the west. The railroad was one of the key reasons Baltimore became a busy ocean port serving the world.

Garrett and his family were well liked. When Maryland's last county was formed in 1872, it was named after this outstanding businessman.

WILLIAM AND HENRY WALTERS

Henry Walters was the son of *William Walters. William was born in Pennsylvania but moved to Baltimore in 1841. William Walters became a very successful merchant and invested in railroads.*

In 1850 he began collecting art. On certain days the Walterses opened their home to anyone who wished to view their beautiful paintings. Henry Walters shared his father's love of art. The two traveled often to Europe to collect art.

Henry Walters was also a suc-cessful businessman. After his father's death, he doubled the family fortune. He added many more art works to the collection begun by his father. He built a beautiful museum to house the art. When Henry Walters died in 1931, the art works and a museum were given to the city of Baltimore. He also left two million dollars for upkeep on the museum.

The Walters Art Gallery remains open today. There are many interesting art objects for people of all ages to enjoy.

Clothing Manufacturing

Manufacturing men's clothing became a big business in 1860. At first there were *sweatshops*. A group of five or six tailors would work together in one small room that was usually very hot. Sometimes one girl would work with them. She would sew on buttons and do other simple tasks. The tailors would work ten to twelve hours a day, six days a week. There were two middlemen between the tailor and the store. The suits made in the sweatshop would be picked up by a man called a "sweater." The sweater would sell the suits to a businessman, who would sell them to stores and shops. Each man had to make a little money from the deal, so that cut down on the amount the tailors got for their work.

Many immigrants worked in sweatshops. They needed jobs and could not speak English. It was hard for them to learn English because they spent most of their days working long hours.

Clothing manufacturing changed when machines were invented. Machines powered by gas or steam were used to do the work. Each machine would do one small job in making a suit. It did not take a lot of skill to do just one thing over and

This kind of sewing machine was used in clothing factories around 1900.

over. Women and children could run the machines. They did not have to be paid as much as the tailors. Soon many factories opened in Baltimore. In 1900 there were 139 manufacturers of men's clothing. One out of every eleven people working in the city was making men's clothing.

Food Canning

The second largest industry in Baltimore was canning fruits, vegetables, and oysters. Harford and other counties close to Baltimore also canned food. In 1900 one-fourth of all food canned in the country was canned in Maryland.

The metal for the cans was made in Baltimore. The labels were printed there too.

Women factory workers opening oysters for canning. This picture appeared in a newspaper in 1873.

Tomatoes, beans, corn, peas, sweet potatoes, succotash, pumpkins, and okra were some of the vegetables canned. Peaches, pears, apples, strawberries, blackberries, raspberries, and cherries were the leading fruits. Many were made into jam and jelly. Tons of sugar was imported to make the jelly.

Oyster canning began in 1820 and grew after 1850. Most of the oysters were sold to China, Japan, and Europe. The shells were ground up and used for fertilizer or as lime.

LEADING BALTIMORE INDUSTRIES				
Year	1870	1880	1890	1900
Men's Clothing	$5,574	$9,447	$15,033	$17,291
Canning Fruit	1,402	5,201	5,723	8,477

Figures are in thousands.   Source: U.S. Census

Work was *seasonal* for many people. This meant they could work only during certain seasons of the year. Most of the vegetables and fruits were *processed* during 100 days in the summer and early fall. Oysters were done during the cooler months. Many of the same people worked in both kinds of canneries. Women and children were often hired for this work.

Tobacco

In 1900 tobacco was the third largest industry in Baltimore. Tobacco was shipped from the farms to the city. The American Tobacco Company was the largest tobacco company there.

Metal Industries

The iron and steel industry played a large part in the rise of factories. Tools and machines were made from iron and steel.

Remains of the Principio Iron Furnace, Cecil County. This picture was taken about 1936.

The Principio Furnace in Cecil County was the largest iron furnace. There came to be less and less iron ore in Maryland. The state bought more of it from Cuba, Spain, and Algiers. It was cheaper to ship it across the Atlantic Ocean than to bring it by train from the middle United States.

Copper ore was imported from Chile and Cuba. It was *smelted* in Baltimore mills and made into bars. Then it was shipped to other places to be made into finished products.

The Baltimore steel mills also designed and built parts of bridges. The parts were sent to Norway, Australia, India, and Japan. The bridges were then put together on the spots where they would stand.

The Marine Railway and Dry Dock Company was operated by Isaac Myers in 1868. Myers was a free-born black. Workers seen in this picture are repairing ships.

Shipping

Shipbuilding also changed during the late 1800s. Metal was now replacing wood for many kinds of ships. Shipbuilding and the steel industry were joined in the 1890s when the Maryland Steel Company built a shipyard at Sparrows Point. The first oil tank steamship was built there. Shipbuilding and steel have been a large part of the business in Baltimore ever since.

Sailing ships were still used into the 1900s. They were cheaper to run. They carried fruits and vegetables, lumber, and other goods on the Chesapeake Bay. Schooners were a common sight around Baltimore in the 1930s. The sleek clippers made for use in the coffee trade set new speed records. The *Josephine II* set an all-time record in 1897. It sailed from Rio de Janeiro to Baltimore in 24 days, 13 hours.

Steamboats were used to carry freight and passengers on the bay. Tobacco, lumber, fertilizer, and seafood were often carried on the bay steamers. There was much competition between steamship companies.

The *Emma Giles* was one of the best-known steamboats. It was built in Baltimore in 1887. The Tolchester Line used the *Emma Giles* to carry thousands of passengers to the Tolchester Beach on the Eastern Shore. As many as 20,000 people a day would take the two-hour trip. The beach, amusement park, and boat ride made for a favorite outing among Baltimoreans until automobiles came along in the 1900s. The steamboat age was at its peak in about 1913, 100 years after it began.

Canal boats were built in Cumberland. Boats of other kinds were built in towns all around the Chesapeake Bay.

Most shipyards were owned by big companies. Smaller ones were privately owned. The Chesapeake Marine Railway and Dry Dock Company was owned by blacks. This company was founded by Isaac Myers.

Cotton Trade

Bales of cotton came by steamship from the South. Huge cotton presses in the port crushed them into smaller bales to save space. These were then shipped to Europe.

Some of the cotton was manufactured in Baltimore. It was made into cotton *duck,* a heavy cloth used for sails. Later, duck was used for awnings, lifeboat covers, and other things.

Cotton was also woven into lighter cloth for sheets and clothing. Twine and yarn also were made here. Twine for fishing nets was used here and also sold abroad.

Fish Industry

Fish and seafood have always been important in the state. This business grew as transportation improved. Because seafood spoils quickly, it needs to be kept cold. With faster trains and ships, seafood could be carried farther before the ice melted.

Crisfield became known as the seafood capital of the world. Crabs, oysters, clams, and fish were all favorite seafoods of Marylanders. The biggest seafood centers were Smith Island, Deal Island, Tilghman Island, Cambridge, Rock Hall, Baltimore, Annapolis, Solomons, and Rock Point. Seafood from the Chesapeake Bay was served in the finest restaurants all over the eastern United States.

Other Products

Maryland farmers learned the value of fertilizers in the early 1800s. The fertilizer industry grew rapidly in the late 1800s. Several other things that have long been made in Baltimore are umbrellas, straw hats, and rye whisky.

New Power Sources

During the late 1800s there was a big change in factories. Products were now being made in large numbers with the help of steam, gas, and water power. Products were no longer being made by hand. Electric motors came a few years later.

Problems of Growth

Many problems came along with the rapid growth of Baltimore. Baltimore faced the same troubles as other industrial cities.

Unloading oysters from the ship. This photograph was taken in Baltimore in 1905. What do you see in this picture that you might not see in Baltimore today?

Pay was very poor for workers in the factories and sweatshops. Most of them worked ten to twelve hours a day, six days a week. Children worked too. There were many children under twelve working in the canneries and clothing factories. Some children started to work full-time at the age of eight. In 1900 five out of every 100 workers were children. Many factories were hot and stuffy and did not have enough light. The big machines could be dangerous.

Low Wages, Child Labor, Health Problems

In the 1800s the *sewers* in Baltimore were used only for collecting storm run-off water. Kitchen waste and laundry water were thrown into the gutters.

Some houses had indoor bathrooms, but they did not connect to sewer lines. They emptied into *cesspools*. This caused the ground to be soaked. The cesspools were cleaned out once in a while, but the ground around them remained wet. Waste from outhouses was picked up and removed by wagons.

In the warm months there was a daily garbage and ash pickup to keep the smell down. In the colder months garbage was picked up only three times a week.

There was much illness in all cities. Many people could not pay for a doctor's care. Hundreds died of tuberculosis, a lung disease that is easily spread. It was the number one cause of death in 1900.

Crowded Housing

Baltimore was very crowded. It could not keep up with the

Some immigrants lived in crowded, run-down housing. Times were very hard.

fast-growing population.

Houses were built in rows, all joined together. They had windows in the front and back. Few had any yard in the front. They had very small back yards. An alley ran through the middle of many city blocks. The back yard faced the alley.

In some cases many people were crowded in one room. A family would rent one or two rooms in a *tenement* building with many other people. The tenements had dim lights and not enough fresh air. There were no water or sewer systems.

ROW HOUSES

T he row house is a symbol of Baltimore and several other East Coast cities. In Baltimore the owner bought the house but only rented the land. This kept the price lower. It helped many people become homeowners. Many bought the land when they finished paying for the house.

All of the houses in one neighborhood were built alike. Different neighborhoods had different style row houses. Some had large bay windows, porches, or were three or four stories high. Some had a rear building for servants and for work areas.

The kitchen in the early houses was separate. There were fireplaces for heat. When coal and gas stoves came along, kitchens were moved inside. There was less danger of fire. Furnaces later made the houses more pleasant and safe.

Thousands of row houses were built in the late 1800s and early 1900s. They often had marble trim on the windows and marble steps in the front. They were two stories high with a basement.

These run-down row houses were made into bath houses in the 1900s. It is likely that immigrants first lived here in the 1800s. These buildings are made of wood. Many of the row houses were made of brick.

MARIE NAGLE'S LIFE IN A ROW HOUSE

The year is 1880. Marie Nagle is eleven years old. She lives in a red brick row house in south Baltimore. Her family is not wealthy but not as poor as many others.

Marie's grandfather, Frank Nagle, came from Germany in 1843. He was 22 years old. He married a young lady from Germany. She had come to the United States with her family. The Nagles had three sons and Marie. Only one son lived past the age of two.

Marie's father works in a dye works. There cloth is dyed many colors. He works ten hours a day, six days a week. Marie's mother works at home sewing designs on gloves and shawls. The work is brought to her by a contractor. He pays a certain amount for each piece she makes. She sews many hours each day and in the evenings, too. Marie does much of the housework so her mother can sew.

There are many chores Marie must do today so the house will look clean. They want to rent out the middle bedroom, and a man is coming to see it. The hall runner must be rolled up and taken outside to be beaten. The wire rug beater has a handle and is shaped like a tennis racket. Marie must also clean the gas lamps. She hates to clean those dirty, smelly things. She also needs to empty the drip pan from the icebox before it runs over. That is a messy job. She hears the ice man shouting from the street. Her mother left enough money for twenty pounds.

The back yard is always damp and smelly. The Nagles have indoor plumbing, but there is no sewer system. The sewage goes to an underground cesspool. It must be pumped out several times a year. Too many houses with too many people use the same cesspool. That is why the ground stays damp.

The Nagles are thinking about Marie going to work in one of the mills. Mama says it's better that she stay home and learn to do fine embroidery work. She fears Marie might die of consumption if she works in the mills. Mama's sister did. Papa says it's not the mills. Aunt Gertrude had consumption and she never worked in a mill.

The Nagle family is going on the horse cars to the German American Society picnic tomorrow. There will be music, games, and food. The Athletic Club will put on a show. Marie hopes there will be ice cream.

People Work to Make Changes

The city government did not seem to be working for the good of the people. For this cause, a group of citizens formed the Reform League to change the government. The *Baltimore Evening News* wrote about the terrible conditions in the *slums*. The *Baltimore Sun* newspaper joined the fight for better government in the city and the state.

Doctors at Johns Hopkins University School of Medicine were leaders in forming the Maryland Public Health Association. Their names are William Osler, William Welsh, William Halsted, and Howard A. Kelly. They saw the importance of eating the proper food and getting plenty of fresh air. They also felt that better conditions at work and home, plus shorter work hours, were needed for better health. They began an organization to fight tuberculosis. Today it is known as the American Lung Association.

JOHNS HOPKINS, 1795-1873

Johns Hopkins was born in Anne Arundel County. He became a very rich man. He lived most of his life in Baltimore. He never married.

Upon his death, Johns Hopkins left money for a university. It was the first university in America for research and discovering new information about the world. Other universities were only interested in educating students. Hopkins also gave his country home, known as Clifton, to the university as a gift.

In 1901 the city of Baltimore bought Clifton. Johns Hopkins University was then moved to Charles Street.

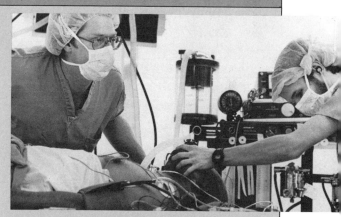

This patient at Johns Hopkins Hospital is having surgery. When people have major surgery they are put to sleep by special drugs called anesthetics. Here, a patient breathes anesthetic gases through a rubber mask. The gases make him fall asleep and keep him from feeling pain. Do you know of another way people are given anesthetics?

Johns Hopkins also left money for a hospital. Today people from all over the world receive care at Johns Hopkins Hospital. Many wonderful discoveries have been made there. Radium treatment for cancer was begun there. In 1973 a long-term pacemaker for heart patients was developed at Johns Hopkins. More recently, this hospital pioneered laser surgery.

There were few open spaces in the crowded parts of Baltimore where the poor people lived. There was a need for places where children could play outdoors and where everyone could enjoy outdoor games. In 1902 the city began to build parks.

FREDERICK LAW OLMSTED, 1822-1903

Frederick Law Olmsted was a landscape architect. He designed large parks and small cities. He was the planner of Sudbrook near Pikesville. He planned a neighborhood with gardens, curved streets, golf course, pool, and a park. It was one of the earliest planned communities in the country.

Olmsted also helped plan the neighborhood of Roland Park. It was the first to have a shopping center. It had an electric streetcar line that went from City Hall to Roland Park. The Olmsted brothers followed their father's ideas about fresh air, light, and using the natural beauty of the land. Frederick Olmsted tried to use the natural scenery without destroying it. His idea was to create rural settings in the heart of big cities. He is perhaps best known for his parks on the grounds of the U.S. Capitol in Washington, D.C.

His son, Frederick Law Olmsted, Jr., followed in his father's footsteps. He served on the National Capital Park and Planning Commission in Washington, D.C. He also taught landscape architecture at Harvard University.

The leaders of Maryland agreed, on February 6, 1904, to improve the cities by improving the parks, sewers, roads, schools, and firehouses. The next day, 70 blocks of Baltimore

The cold weather did not help the brave firemen fight the great fire in Baltimore, 1904.

Baltimore and Ohio Railroad Strike, 1877. This was one way workers tried to get better pay and working conditions. What is happening in the picture?

near the harbor were destroyed by fire. More than 1,200 firemen worked to put out the blaze. It lasted over 30 hours. Finally, the wind shifted and the fire was driven into the water. More than 1,500 buildings holding over 2,500 businesses were in ashes. Happily, no one was killed in the fire. People worked to rebuild the city within about two years.

Unions Begin

Labor unions began to be formed in 1866. Unions were made up of people who joined together to try to get better conditions and pay for workers. They tried to get laws passed against sweatshops. Unions gained higher pay for their members over the years.

Laws Help Bring Changes

In 1906 Maryland government passed laws that said children under age twelve could not work in the factories. Later the law was changed to age fourteen.

Maryland's first hospital for tuberculosis was opened. Anyone with the disease had to register with the Public Health Department.

Even the row houses changed. Many were still two-story red brick, but they were wider. The floor plan was changed so that each room had a window. These were called sunshine houses.

All of the changes you have read about continued into the early 1900s. It was a time when more people adjusted to living in the cities. Just as in the early 1600s, a great number of people were new to this country.

STUDY

WORDS TO KNOW

bale	planned community
cannery	process
cesspool	seasonal
consumption	sewer system
contractor	slum
developer	smelt
labor union	sweat shop
landscape architect	tenement

QUESTIONS TO ANSWER

1. When did the population of Maryland reach one million?
2. After 1900, what four things replaced farming as the state's important industries?
3. Name three things John Garrett did to improve railroads in Maryland.
4. Describe a sweatshop.
5. In 1900, how many people in Baltimore had jobs making men's clothing?
6. In 1900, what fraction of all food canned in the country was canned in Maryland?
7. Where was Maryland's largest iron furnace located? What was its name?
8. What was the biggest change in shipbuilding in the late 1800s?
9. What city became known as the seafood capital of the world?
10. What kind of house became popular in the late 1800s and early 1900s?
11. Who left money for a university upon his death?
12. When did labor unions begin?

INTERPRETING WHAT YOU HAVE READ

13. How did clothing manufacturing change when machines were invented?
14. What product joined the South and Maryland in manufacturing?
15. What were four problems that came when Baltimore grew rapidly?

THINGS TO DISCUSS

16. Compare and contrast the houses of the early 1900s with houses in your neighborhood.
17. Would you say Maryland has solved all its growth problems? Explain.

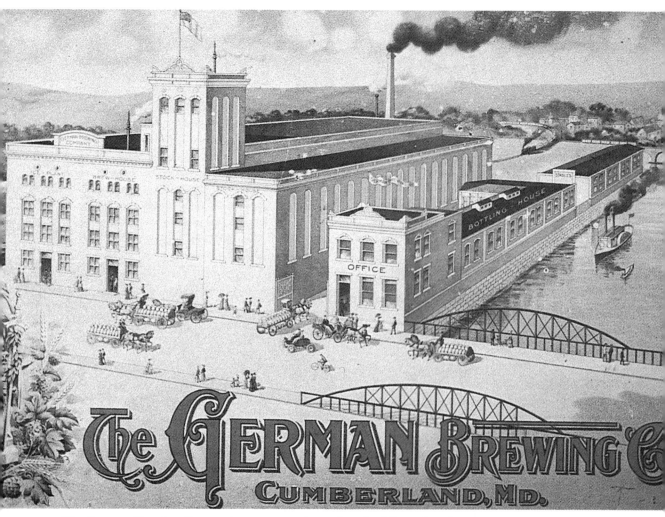

*The German Brewing Company's name was changed to the Liberty Brewing
Company during World War I.*

A Time of Turmoil and Change, 1914-1939

World War I Begins

At this time in history America was concerned with happenings at home. They were only interested in the Western Hemisphere. Not much attention was being paid to Europe.

Many European countries, meanwhile, were ruled by kings or emperors. They had large armies and navies and kept building them larger and stronger. They looked for ways to get more land.

A great feeling began to grow in these countries. They wanted a separate national government in a country where everyone spoke the same language. European countries always competed for colonies and other land. Some countries whose people had almost the same feelings and interests grouped together.

To protect their interests, Great Britain, France, and Russia grouped together. They were called the *Allies*. Germany, Austria-Hungary, and Turkey were called the *Central Powers*.

On June 28, 1914, a single act started a war between the two great powers. Archduke Francis Ferdinand and his wife, Sophie, were killed. They were making a visit in Austria where one day they would have been king and queen. By October 30, 1914, the Central Powers were at war with the Allies. It was known as World War I.

As the years passed, World War I in Europe went on. The United States found it harder and harder not to take sides. They wanted to stay *neutral*.

When the Germans began attacking ships with their submarines, American lives were lost. One passenger ship, the *Lusitania,* was attacked and sunk. There were 128 Americans on the ship. This was the most lives lost at one time. Finally, the United States entered the war. Congress declared war to make the world "safe for democracy." All young men had to sign up for the armed forces.

Before the United States entered the war, Baltimore felt its effects. Large orders of factory goods and food were shipped from Baltimore to Europe. A great deal of the shipments went to Germany. Many people living in Baltimore and nearby counties were German. This made Germany a center of interest for Baltimore.

Feelings Against Germans

Some Marylanders became *suspicious* of the many German immigrants around them. They believed German spies were everywhere. Even the German people who had become U.S. citizens were treated harshly. A street named German Avenue in Baltimore was changed to Redwood Street.

When bombs were found near a Baltimore weapons factory, guards were placed on duty. On April 6, 1917, the first act of war in Baltimore took place. Three German ships were anchored in the harbor. The ships, which were worth a great deal of money, were taken over by the United States.

Field Units

Men and women signed up for service. Some men didn't wait for the United States to enter the war. They had already joined the armies of England, France, and Canada. Maryland men served during World War I in groups that received high honors. These groups were the Rainbow Division of the 117th Field French Mortar Battery and the 115th Regiment of the 29th Division of the army. Most of the men in the 313th Regiment of the 79th Division were from Maryland. The group was known as "Baltimore's Own."

Doctors and nurses from Johns Hopkins Hospital and the University of Maryland formed base hospitals. These were the 18th and the 42nd base hospitals, both in France.

Support from the Home Front

People at home were working hard together to help win World War I. One day a week they went without meat, sugar, and white bread. This was so the people in the service would have more food.

Marylanders sent clothing to the homeless in Europe. They bought Liberty Bonds from the government. Maryland factories made chemicals, steel, weapons, and ships for the war.

During the war new army bases were built in Maryland. The United States Army built the Aberdeen Proving Grounds. It was the first weapons testing center to be built along the Chesapeake Bay. Edgewood Arsenal, next to the Aberdeen Proving Grounds, was also completed during this time. Fort George Meade, near Odenton, was also built. Indian Head, in Charles County, supplied gunpowder. Camp Holabird was a chief supply *depot* for sending tanks and trucks to the battlefields.

These cavalrymen pose in their new uniforms at Fort George Meade.

This is one of the first utility trucks. The picture was taken in 1923. The truck was owned by the Baltimore Gas and Electric Company.

Automobiles in the War

The automobile changed the way men fought during the war. Armored cars were used for the first time. Also for the first time, trucks were used to carry soldiers to the battle fronts. Factories were busy building trucks and tractors. In 1914 the United States was fifteenth in the automobile industry. By 1917 it was seventh. The war ended in 1918.

The automobile became the major means of transportation after the war. As time went on, improvements were made in cars. Before the war, the car was thought to be a *luxury*. After the war, it became more of a *necessity*.

Until the 1920s, most drivers were men. Gasoline-driven cars had to be hand-cranked to start. It was hard to do and quite dangerous. This kept women from driving autos with

Miller Garage, Grantsville, around 1920. The increased use of automobiles meant more gas stations and repair garages were needed.

gasoline engines. When the electric starter came along, many women began to drive. Car sales boomed. The romance between people and cars began to grow.

The first cars had no roofs or windows. There was little protection from wind, dust, rain, or snow. After 1929 most cars had roofs and windows.

Making Automobiles Quickly

Ransom Olds first started the *assembly line*. A car in his plant was placed on a wooden platform. The platform moved along on rollers like wheels on roller skates. As the car's *framework* moved along, men would add parts to it. This went on until the car was finished.

Henry M. Leland led in the development of *interchangeable* parts. This meant parts from one Oldsmobile could be used in another Oldsmobile.

Henry Ford made cars available to more people by using the *conveyor belt*. The moving belt carried parts, as well as the automobile, to the workers. Before the conveyor belt, it took 1½ days to build one car. With a conveyor belt, a car could be put together in 93 minutes. Cars then cost less because they could be made faster. More people could afford them.

Auto Improvements

During the late 1920s and 1930s, balloon tires made riding much smoother. Heaters made cars comfortable in winter. Improved headlights made night driving safer. *Automatic transmissions* made driving much easier.

The car gave many people freedom to travel. The car was not on a route like a streetcar was. Cars could go anywhere there were roads. Cars were thought to be cleaner, safer, and more dependable than horses. Cars also needed less care than horses, and cars were faster.

As more and more people got automobiles, there was a need for better roads on which to drive. In Maryland, two major roads were upgraded and paved. The old National Pike became known as Route 40. Route 1 was still the main road between Baltimore and Washington, D.C.

The trolley car was an important way for people to get around the city. This early picture of Baltimore shows the trolley in the middle of the street. It was powered by electricity. Can you see how the electricity came to the car?

Trolley Cars

The trolley car also became very important. It ran on electricity from an overhead wire. The trolley helped suburbs grow up. People could live farther from their jobs. The trolley was a dependable, cheap way to get to work or to go shopping. As more cars were used, fewer people rode the trolleys.

ROBERT EAGEN, A TYPICAL YOUTH

Robert Eagen was like other fourth graders living in Maryland at the end of World War I in 1918. His father rode the trolley to work in Washington, D.C., where he worked at the navy yard. Bob's mother kept house and helped his grandmother part time in her store. His grandmother had a small grocery store in the front room of the house. She was also a midwife. She worked with a doctor to help bring babies into the world.

Bob's family used kerosene lamps and had a well for water in the back yard. They also had an out-house. By the time Bob was fifteen, the family had moved to another house that had electricity. His father was not well enough to work all day, so his mother went to work in a bakery.

Bob quit school. He became a helper to a plumber so he could learn a trade. Plumbing was a good field of work. All new homes were being built with indoor toilets and sinks. Running water and bathrooms were being added to older homes.

While growing up, Bob had many jobs at home. He had to keep wood and coal in the house for stoves. He also had a paper route. He picked up newspapers at the trolley stop on his way home. He delivered his bundles of papers to the barber shop, the drug store, the grocery store, and other businesses. Only a few of his customers had home delivery.

Many people had no transportation other than the trolley. They would bring large packages from the city on the trolley. Bob would meet these people at the trolley stop and haul the packages the rest of the way home in his wagon. He carried blocks of ice, groceries, and even bushels of coal. He was paid for doing this. There was no set price. Customers paid what they wished, with some giving more than others.

Grandmother would go to the city and buy things to be sold in her little store. Bob had to be at the trolley on time to meet her. He was not paid for hauling Grandmother's packages. Instead, she gave him some of the hard candy she carried in her purse. He hoped she didn't arrive on the same trolley with some of his paying customers. It was a family rule that he had to pull her things home first.

During July and August, Bob worked at Chesapeake Beach in Calvert County. He helped in the kitchen and ran errands for the hotel owner. He cranked the ice cream freezer for the desserts. Washing, peeling, and cutting up vegetables was also part of

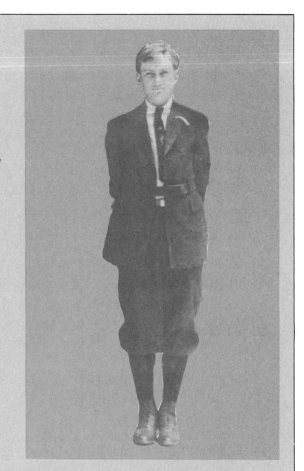

his job. Sometimes he washed the dishes or cleaned fish caught by the guests.

Listening to the crystal set (early radio) with Mr. Loff on the weekends was a nice treat. They could hear Pittsburgh quite often. On a particularly clear night they could even tune in Havana, Cuba.

Bob attended church each week with his family. Several times during the summer there would be "tent meetings." There, traveling ministers would preach and the people would sing all afternoon under the large, tan tent. Everyone would go home for dinner and return for the evening service. Some families brought a picnic lunch.

Bob would rather have been at the baseball field in the afternoon. The Maryland Aces were a good team. It seemed to him that they were always playing at home on tent-meeting Sundays.

Airplanes Improve Transportation

The airplane was another kind of transportation which made giant steps during the early 1900s. The Wright brothers' flight at Kitty Hawk, North Carolina, made others want to fly. In the early 1900s pilots risked their lives to set records. They knew very little about flying or the effects of weather.

When World War I began, airplanes had open framework bodies. During the war airplanes were designed and built better. Glenn L. Martin made bombers in 1918. Donald W. Douglas started his own airplane company.

College Park, Maryland, is the home of the first general air field in the world. The Wright brothers flew airplanes there. College Park was also where early helicopter experiments took place.

Experimenting with flight was not new to Marylanders. After the Revolutionary War, the first balloon flights in

Henry Berliner and his son, Emile, did helicopter experiments at the College Park Airport beginning in 1920. Theirs was the first machine that could be controlled while in the air. This picture shows Henry at the controls of the 1920 Model C.

America took place in Bladensburg and Baltimore. Ten-year-old Edward Warren became the first American to travel through the air. He boarded a balloon for a flight over today's Mt. Vernon Place in Baltimore.

War Ends

In November 1918, after four bitter years of fighting, World War I ended. Germany asked for an end to the war. That country had lost more people than any other country in the war.

Germany was forced to give up land to the Allies. It also had to pay for part of the cost of the war. Czechoslovakia and Poland were two countries that were created from this land. Now they would be independent countries that would govern themselves.

Prohibition

In 1919 the U.S. Congress passed a law against making or selling alcoholic beverages. This was known as *prohibition*. *Bootleggers* made whisky in their basements or barns anyway. Underworld gangs bought it from them and sold it on the sly. The gangs fought each other for larger territories. There was bloodshed in the streets. The violence during this time gave the 1920s an odd name. It was called the Roaring Twenties. This name also came about because people were having a lot of fun and happy times.

Two young women in the latest style swimsuits are ready for a swim in the C & O Canal in the early 1920s.

These women are working at the Gold Dust Soap Factory in Baltimore about 1920.

Like people across the country, Marylanders did not like prohibition. They believed that it was the state's right to decide such matters. It was at this time that Maryland got the nickname "Free State." Maryland's Governor Albert Ritchie was a leader in the fight to keep the states free to make their own decisions.

Changes for Women

During the 1920s another change was taking place. Women were beginning to work outside of the home. They became more independent. *Suffragists* worked to get women the right to vote. Finally in 1920, the U.S. government gave all women in the country this right.

Stock Market Crash

In the early 1920s many people had money. Thousands bought *shares* of *stock* in companies. A share is a part. A stock is a piece of paper that says a person owns a part of a company. People who owned these shares hoped to sell them later at a higher price. They would make a big *profit* this way. A large company could have hundreds of *stockholders*.

In the late 1920s companies began to make more goods than they could sell. Many of these companies had taken out bank loans to build new buildings or add on to their businesses in other ways. When their goods did not sell fast, they had to lower the prices so people would buy them. This did not work very well, though, and soon the value of stocks went down.

In 1929 prices in the *stock market* fell fast. Within a few days people all over the United States lost their money. Businesses and people could not pay back their bank loans, and many banks failed. The stock market "crash" hurt everyone.

The Great Depression

The years following the stock market crash were called the Great Depression. *Depression* means a low point. The years from 1929 to 1940 were a low point for the American people. Thousands lost their jobs. People had little money. Many lost their homes. Many men who moved from place to place to find jobs had to depend on the kindness of others for food. These men were called hobos or tramps. If they couldn't find work, they would knock on doors asking for food. To help his friends, a hobo would somehow mark a house where he got food. Then others would know where to get a handout.

Sometimes whole families traveled from farm to farm.

As many people who could raised some of their own food during the Great Depression. Here a farmer and his wife are preparing to butcher a hog. What kinds of food might this pig give them?

Eleven people of one family lived in this log cabin in western Maryland during the Great Depression. What kinds of problems do you think they had living together?

They would harvest the crops that the farmers grew. They mostly picked crops that would be sent to canneries. Their pay was very low. Living conditions were poor.

People raised as much of their own food as they could. Animals were raised for meat. Housewives raised gardens and canned as much food as they could.

Many families had to ask for help during this time. They needed food, clothes, and homes. Churches and ladies groups opened "soup kitchens." This was a place where people could get a free meal of soup and bread.

Roosevelt's New Deal

In 1933 Franklin D. Roosevelt was voted into the office of president. President Roosevelt had a new plan to give people jobs. It was called the New Deal. The government would hire people to build roads, bridges, and buildings. There would be jobs cleaning campgrounds and making new trails in the forests. These and other kinds of jobs would help to solve the problems of the depression.

Some people did not think the New Deal would work. They said people would expect to get high pay for unskilled jobs. Others said the people would want to get public relief payments without doing any work.

In Maryland the plan had a good effect. Government projects of the Public Works Administration (PWA), the Civil Works Administration (CWA), and the Works Progress Administration (WPA) hired thousands of Marylanders. The New Deal was working. By 1940 better times had returned to Maryland and the rest of the country.

STUDY

WORDS TO KNOW

assembly line	depression
automatic transmission	framework
bootlegger	interchangeable
conveyor belt	kerosene
depot	luxury

midwife	stockholder
necessity	stock market
prohibition	suffragist
share	suspicious
stock	welfare

QUESTIONS TO ANSWER

1. Why was Germany a center of interest for Baltimore during World War I?
2. Name three ways Marylanders helped in World War I.
3. What invention allowed many more women to drive?
4. Name four other changes that improved automobiles in the late 1920s and 1930s.
5. How did the trolley help the suburbs grow?
6. What part did College Park play in air travel improvement?
7. What United States law in 1919 was unpopular in Maryland?
8. When were all women given the right to vote?
9. What were the ten years following the stock market crash called?
10. Who helped people with food, clothing, and jobs during the Great Depression?
11. What was the name of Franklin D. Roosevelt's plan to put money back into peoples' pockets?

INTERPRETING WHAT YOU HAVE READ

12. Did Maryland's economy grow or shrink because of World War I?
13. How did Maryland get the nickname "Free State"?

THINGS TO DISCUSS

14. How is your life different from Robert Eagen's? How is it like his?

This woman worked in Fairchild Aircraft plant in Hagerstown, during World War II. It was the first time women had done this kind of work.

Maryland in its Fourth Century, 1940 to the Present

World War II

The depression was not only in the United States and Maryland. It was worldwide. Some countries in Europe tried to solve their problems by invading neighboring countries. Adolf Hitler of Germany and Benito Mussolini of Italy were the invaders. They plunged Europe into war in 1939. World War II began.

For Americans and Marylanders, World War II did not begin until December 7, 1941. Japan attacked the American naval base at Pearl Harbor, Hawaii. We had no choice; we had to fight. In this war, the United States, England, France, and Russia were the Allies. Germany, Italy, and Japan were the Axis powers.

Maryland's Part in the War

Maryland once again got busy making needed war goods. Factory workers were needed again. All of Maryland, and especially Baltimore, began a new time of growth. Workers from the *Appalachian* area, the South, and from other states came to Baltimore. There were plenty of jobs. The Baltimore shipyards built more than 600 large ships. Small boats were built for both the army and navy. Thousands of planes were put together in plants in and around Baltimore.

GLENN L. MARTIN, 1886-1955

Glenn L. Martin was always interested in flying. He flew for the first time in 1909 in an airplane he had designed and built himself. By 1911 he had become one of the best-known fliers in the United States. He worked with many airplane companies. At one time he was in partnership with the Wright brothers.

During World War II the Glenn L. Martin Aircraft Company in Baltimore built many of the airplanes used in Europe. Martin directed the making of bombers and sea planes used to defend American soldiers.

Glen L. Martin inspects a model of one of his airplanes. His company moved to Middle River, outside of Baltimore, in 1929.

Counties in Maryland helped in the war in different ways. The navy manufactured much of its gunpowder at the Naval Powder Factory in Charles County. All maps used by the army were prepared in Montgomery County. This county also had the National Medical Center, a hospital and *research* center. The Navy *Hydrographic* Office in Prince George's County prepared charts for the navy. Andrews Air Force Base was opened in Prince George's County.

Military Bases

In Anne Arundel County, navy officers were trained at Annapolis. Soldiers were trained at Fort George Meade. Thousands of sailors were trained at Bainbridge in Cecil County. Weapons were tested for the army in Aberdeen, Harford County. There was also a depot in this county for weapons used in *chemical warfare*. Camp Detrich, in Frederick County, studied germ warfare. The Patuxent Naval Air Test Center in St. Mary's County tested planes needed for victory in the Pacific Ocean.

Nurses and Doctors Serve

The 18th and the 118th hospitals were formed by doctors and nurses at Johns Hopkins. They served in Australia, Burma, and islands of the Pacific Ocean. The University of Maryland Medical School made up the 42nd and 142nd general hospitals. Doctors and nurses from the school served in Australia, Japan, and the Pacific islands. Other Maryland medical people served in England, Belgium, and France. They were with the 56th General Hospital.

Farmers Do Their Part

The farmers of Maryland were also doing their part. They grew tons of meat and vegetables. Their soybean crop was three times as big as in past years. Maryland canneries sold canned meats, seafood, and vegetables to the army and navy. Fourteen canneries and meat packers received awards for their work.

The U.S. Naval Academy in Annapolis prepared young men for military service during World War II. Hundreds of men and women try to get accepted to Annapolis each year.

Women took over the jobs of men who had gone to war. These women are keeping the trains of the B & O Railroad clean and in good running order.

Women's Role

Since men had to go to war, women replaced them in the work place. Women worked in all of the factories. They became streetcar conductors and bus and taxi drivers. Many women joined the armed services. A special group of women pilots flew planes overseas for use in the war. Women did many other jobs at home and in the armed services.

Women of all ages helped the war effort. They made food and held dances and stage shows for servicemen and servicewomen at the United Services Organization (USO) building.

This helped keep the men and women from getting homesick. Many people in the service were a long way from home for the first time. The shows by movie stars and local performers cheered up the young people in the service.

World War II Ends

The war in Europe ended in May 1945. The war with Japan did not end until August 1945. It had been a long and cruel war. Many lives had been lost. Hitler and Mussolini were dead.

After the war the Allies built army bases in Germany, Italy, and Japan. Many allied soldiers remained there. This kept these countries from trying to start another war.

Marylanders looked forward to a time of peace.

Post-War Growth

Maryland kept growing rapidly after the war was over. Great changes were made in transportation. More than 1,100 miles of new roads were built in four years. The Baltimore-Washington Parkway and the Annapolis-Washington road (Route 50) were built. A road connecting Baltimore and Harrisburg, Pennsylvania, was finished. Beltways around the cities of Washington and Baltimore were added.

A bridge across the Chesapeake Bay was opened in 1952. This connected the Eastern Shore with the rest of Maryland. Up until this time, a trip on a ferry boat was the only way to cross the bay. The Baltimore airport was moved from the city to the suburbs. Friendship Airport, now called Baltimore-Washington International, was built in Anne Arundel County.

With travel made easy, Marylanders took trips for fun. They had money and time to get away from home for a few days each year.

The whole East Coast was growing. A long strip of cities is called a *megalopolis* (meg-uh-LOP-oh-lis). Maryland is part of a megalopolis that stretches from Richmond, Virginia, to Boston, Massachusetts. Different kinds of transportation make it easy for people to travel from one place to another.

Integration in the Schools

Changes were also taking place in education. Until the 1950s black and white students attended separate schools. This is called *segregation*. Black students often had to ride buses a long way to school. A law kept black and white students from attending school together. This was because of *prejudice*. This means having bad feelings toward someone without a real cause.

Martin Luther King, Jr., was a national leader who worked for black rights. He worked to change more laws. As a result, black and white people were mixed together in schools in 1954. This was called *integration*. The two races had a chance to better understand each other.

THURGOOD MARSHALL, BLACK LEADER

Thurgood Marshall was born in Baltimore in 1908. He graduated from Lincoln University. He studied law at Howard University in Washington, D.C., and began practicing law in 1933.

Marshall worked on the legal case that brought about the 1954 Supreme Court decision making racial *segregation* unconstitutional. He served as chief counsel for the National Association for the Advancement of Colored People (NAACP) from 1938 to 1961.

Thurgood Marshall became the first black to serve as an associate justice of the United States Supreme Court. He was called to that post by President Lyndon Johnson.

Thurgood Marshall (left) helped open the University of Maryland to black students. He handled the court case of Donald B. Murray (middle) in 1934. Because Marshall won the case, Murray was allowed to attend the University of Maryland Law School.

The Move to Suburbia

New houses built at this time were the beginning of *suburbia*. Towns such as Joppatowne in Harford County and Bowie in Prince George's County were built. Crofton in Anne Arundel County and the Montgomery Village area of Gaithersburg also sprang up. These places became home for people who worked in Baltimore and Washington.

Columbia in Howard County became a new kind of community. It was planned as a place where people could work as well as live. Industrial parks and office buildings were part of the plan. It is a complete community drawn up by Columbia's developer James Rouse. Schools, open space, community centers, and a shopping mall were also part of the plan.

Columbia has attracted people from the middle classes. It has a greater mix of people from different economic and ethnic backgrounds than other suburban communities.

Medical center at Greenbelt. Greenbelt was another planned community. It had schools, stores, and homes, as well as health care centers. How is your community like a planned community? How is it different?

Wars and Protests

Many wonderful changes took place after World War II. The world, however, remained unsettled.

Tension between the United States and Russia seemed to build after World War II. Both countries found it hard to understand one another. The fact that Russia was a communist country did not help.

Russia's influence in Korea brought the United States into another war in 1950. Korea was divided in half. North Korea remained a communistic country. South Korea remained free. Five hundred Marylanders lost their lives in the war. Over 15,000 Koreans made their new home in Maryland. Koreans became Maryland's largest foreign-born ethnic group.

Conflict between communism and democracy flared again in the 1960s. Another war took place in Asia. It was in Vietnam. This was a very unpopular war. Many young citizens became angry about the United States taking part in the war. People in Maryland were divided. Some felt we had no business fighting another country's battle. Others felt we had to fight to protect the world against communism.

Many protests were held at colleges. Students at the University of Maryland staged sit-down demonstrations on Route 1 near the school. People were not able to drive their cars through the crowds of people. At Bowie State College and Maryland University, students held more sit-down demonstrations. Tempers were very hot at these public demonstrations.

Protests reached a peak in 1969 and 1970. *Anti*-war parades were held in Baltimore and Washington. Some young men burned their *draft cards*. They chose to go to jail rather than fight in Vietnam.

In the end, Vietnam became a communist country. The war ended so quickly that many of our country's supplies fell into enemy hands. U.S. soldiers were lucky to get out of the country safely. It is believed that some of our servicemen were held prisoners after the war ended. Maryland again became the home for many Asian families after the war.

This Korean family is gathered for a sixtieth birthday dinner. In the Korean culture the first and sixtieth birthdays are very important. The long table in front holds colored rice cakes and fresh fruits. By carrying on customs like this, Koreans and other ethnic groups can preserve some of their own culture.

Black Protest Peaks

At the peak of the Vietnam trouble, there was a very sad death in our country. Martin Luther King, Jr., was assassinated. The sadness that filled some people caused blind anger in others. There was *looting* and rioting. Buildings were burned in Cambridge and Baltimore.

From this troubled time came new black leadership. These people helped bring order to the angry communities. They worked together for changes in jobs and housing for blacks. Today's leaders follow the fine examples set by earlier black leaders.

LILLIE MAE CARROLL JACKSON, 1889-1975

Lillie Mae Carroll was born in Baltimore on May 25, 1889, one of eight children. Her father, Charles Henry Carroll, was a descendant *of Charles Carroll. Her mother, Amanda Bowen Carroll, was the granddaughter of John Bowen. He was an African chief who was never a slave.*

Lillie Mae Carroll Jackson.

Lillie Mae Carroll received her early education in the public schools of Baltimore. She graduated from Colored High and Training School in 1908. She married Keiffer Jackson. They traveled around the country together, showing religious movies to church groups. Lillie Mae would speak and sing before the movies were shown.

Lillie Mae Jackson believed that home, church, and school had the biggest effects on building a person's character. She taught this idea to her four children. After being married 60 years, her husband died.

Jackson became president of the NAACP when it was founded on May 4, 1912.

In 1931 she and her daughter, Juanita, started a campaign *against* economic *discrimination. Their sign read, "Buy where you can work." They would buy only in places where black people could be hired.*

Jackson also worked to open colleges to black students. She worked for new laws that changed the pay scale for black teachers. In 1938 black teachers' pay was finally equal to that of all teachers in Maryland.

Lillie Mae Jackson's children, following her example, have all led full lives. One daughter is a singer, one a lawyer, and one an artist. Her son is manager of the family's real estate company.

Jackson's home in Baltimore is now a museum.

JUANITA JACKSON MITCHELL

Juanita Jackson Mitchell is the daughter of Lillie Mae Jackson. Juanita graduated from Douglas High School in Baltimore. She earned a law degree from the University of Maryland School of Law. In 1950 she became the first black woman lawyer in the state.

As a lawyer, Mitchell filed suits that brought about the integration of Baltimore City Public Schools. She also won court cases that gave blacks the right to swim at Sandy Point State Beach and Fort Smallwood Beach. She did the same for swimming pools in Baltimore.

Mitchell's husband, Clarence M. Mitchell, Jr., was a noted state senator. He was well known for his leadership in the black civil rights movement. The Mitchells have two sons who hold public office in Maryland.

Juanita Mitchell followed in her mother's footsteps as a leader. She started the NAACP youth movement. Juanita Mitchell also directed the first city-wide register and vote campaign in 1942. She worked for this group through 1960. Her leadership has moved others to make a difference in civil rights today.

Juanita Jackson Mitchell.

Goddard Space Center was opened in 1959. Goddard mainly deals with near earth satellites. Part of their work is tracking and communications for all U.S. spacecraft. Shown in this model is the Apollo 11 *moon landing. Astronaut Neil Armstrong is standing next to the command module. The picture on the wall shows Dr. Robert Goddard with his first rocket.*

1970s Bring Changes in the Work Place

The nuclear power plant in Calvert County first *employed* many workers to build it. Since its opening in 1975, it has had many technical workers.

The Goddard Space Center in Greenbelt also has thousands of *high tech* workers. There are other companies that have contracts with the National Aeronautics and Space Administration (NASA). These companies hire many scientists and engineers.

As Maryland entered the 1970s, still more changes took place. Businesses and government offices changed holiday dates. These changes brought about three-day weekends that we love. As a result, people began to take more short vacations.

This was good for business in tourist towns. A strip of land ten miles long and about three blocks wide became a *boom town*. Ocean City in Worcester County plays host to about 250,000 tourists each summer weekend. Many high-rise apartments have been built in Ocean City.

Tourism

Tourism is a very big business in Maryland. It brings in more money now than ever before.

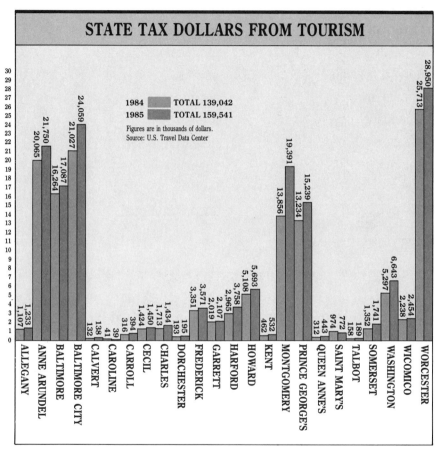

STATE TAX DOLLARS FROM TOURISM

1984 TOTAL 139,042
1985 TOTAL 159,541

Figures are in thousands of dollars.
Source: U.S. Travel Data Center

County	1984	1985
ALLEGANY	1,107	1,233
ANNE ARUNDEL	20,065	21,750
BALTIMORE	16,264	17,087
BALTIMORE CITY	21,027	24,059
CALVERT	132	138
CAROLINE	39	41
CARROLL	316	394
CECIL	1,424	1,450
CHARLES	1,434	1,713
DORCHESTER	193	195
FREDERICK	3,351	3,571
GARRETT	2,019	2,107
HARFORD	2,965	3,758
HOWARD	5,108	5,693
KENT	462	532
MONTGOMERY	13,856	19,391
PRINCE GEORGE'S	13,234	15,239
QUEEN ANNE'S	312	443
SAINT MARY'S	772	974
TALBOT	158	189
SOMERSET	1,352	1,741
WASHINGTON	5,297	6,643
WICOMICO	2,238	2,454
WORCESTER	25,713	28,950

The graph compares state tax dollars received from tourist businesses for two years. The information is broken down by county.

Maryland in the 1980s

As Maryland entered the 1980s, the people got more interested in protecting their environment. Marylanders are also still working for harmony among races. The state's leaders hope to help keep Maryland a good place in which to live and work. Like the rest of the country, we are trying to overcome money and job problems. We are finding better ways to handle the work of government and growth.

STUDY

WORDS TO KNOW

anti (prefix)
Appalachia
boom town
campaign
chemical warfare
communism
descendant
draft card
economic
employ
high tech

hydrographic
integration
loot
megalopolis
neutral
patriotic
prejudice
research
suburbia
tourism
unconstitutional

QUESTIONS TO ANSWER

1. During what years did the United States fight in World War II?

2. What two kinds of transportation did Maryland build for use in World War II?

3. Name three places in Maryland used by the military during World War II.

4. Name four ways women helped in the war effort.

5. What city is at each end of the eastern megalopolis?

6. In 1954, how did schools make it easier for different races to understand each other?

7. What Marylander became the first black to serve as an associate justice of the United States Supreme Court?

8. What two wars was the United States involved in after World War II? How did these wars affect immigration to Maryland?

9. Name a mother and daughter who have been leaders in civil rights.

INTERPRETING WHAT YOU HAVE READ

10. How did World War II change the lives of many women?

11. What would you say are some key words which describe life in Maryland from 1940 to the present?

THINGS TO DISCUSS

12. How did additional roads and bridges change our use of spare time?

13. What place in your county do you feel could be made into a tourist attraction? Explain how this might be done.

The seal of Maryland appears on all official papers.

Government in Maryland

What is Government?

Government is the way people work out rules and laws for living together. Cities, counties, states, and nations all have governments. Governments have the power to see that laws are obeyed. What would life be like without government?

Why We Need Government

Think about the following story.

A rich man gave an acre of land to a community. People began fighting over what to do with this ground. Finally, a group of citizens were picked to make a plan. They decided that a park with a swimming pool would be good for all the people. The community then voted on the plan and it passed. What might have happened if the planning group had not been selected?

Many Levels of Government

We live under rules and laws of many governments. We live under county, state, and federal governments. If we live in a town or city, we also live under that government.

FEDERAL GOVERNMENT	makes decisions for the United States
STATE GOVERNMENT	makes decisions for the state; carries out some federal laws and programs
COUNTY GOVERNMENT	makes decisions for the county; carries out some state and federal programs
MUNICIPAL GOVERNMENT	makes decisions for cities or towns

Political Parties

To be able to serve in most government offices, a person must first be *nominated* (named) by one of the political parties. Parties are organized groups of people who have the same ideas about government. Democrats and Republicans are the major parties. There are also some parties with fewer members. These are called *third parties*.

Each party chooses the best people it can find to run for office. The person selected is called the *candidate*. Some citizens don't belong to any party. They may run for office and vote as *Independents*.

The donkey is the symbol for the Democratic party. The elephant is the Republican symbol.

Voting and Elections

The kind of government our country has is called a *representative democracy*. Through votes, people are chosen to represent a number of citizens. To be able to vote, people must be at least 18 years old, a citizen of the United States, and be *registered* (signed up). They must also have lived in Maryland at least 30 days before the *general election*.

Elections for county, state, and federal offices are held every two years. Different offices have different lengths of service. The United States President and the Governor of Maryland serve a four-year term. The United States House of Representatives and the Maryland General Assembly members serve a two-year term. United States Senators serve a six-year term.

In September the *primary* election is held to select candidates from each party. Citizens registered as Republicans choose from among Republican candidates. Democrats choose from among Democrats. The winners of the primary election from each party run against the winners from the other parties in the *general election* in November.

ROLE PLAYING

ACTIVITY

Let's find out how representative democracy works. As a class, choose one of these subjects to talk about:

1. **Should Maryland allow children to be taught at home instead of at school?**

2. **Should a second nuclear power plant be built in Maryland?**

3. **Should a subway be built between Baltimore and Annapolis?**

Divide into small groups. Share ideas on the subject you chose. Talk about the good and bad points of your ideas. Take a vote to see which idea your group favors. Vote to choose one or two people to represent your group.

Representatives from all the groups should then talk about the subject. Each representative should present his or her group's ideas. Then the representatives will vote for the best ideas. You will have taken part in a representative democracy.

Taking Part in Government

There are many things a citizen can do to make a representative government work well. Voting and working for a political party are two ways. You can also let your elected representatives know your feeling on certain laws or issues. A person of any age can send a letter of thanks to them for doing a good job. Letters show that you are interested in what is happening. You can listen to the radio, watch TV, and read newspapers to become a well informed citizen. It is helpful to know what is going on in government. That will give you a better background to judge what is best for all the people. You will be able to vote for the best candidate for each office.

ACTIVITY

QUALITIES FOR LEADERSHIP

Below is a list of things one person thought made him a good candidate for the Maryland Senate. Divide into groups. Talk over each point. Which ones do you and the members of your group think would help make a good state senator?

1. **College graduate**

2. **Two years in the army**

3. **Six years as a school teacher**

4. **Twelve years as a business owner**

5. **Six years as a scout leader**

6. **Active in church and P.T.A.**

7. **Past president of Rotary Club**

Maryland Constitution

A constitution is an official set of rules for the government. It also gives citizens rights. The men who wrote Maryland's first constitution in 1776 wanted to guarantee many rights for the people. Listed below are some:

- **Freedom to worship as one chooses**
- **Freedom of speech**
- **Freedom of the press**
- **Trial by jury**

The state constitution also sets the plan for three branches, or parts, of government. They are the legislative, executive, and judicial branches. Each branch has a certain job to do. They cannot do each other's jobs. This is called the separation of powers. This way no single branch or person can gain too much power.

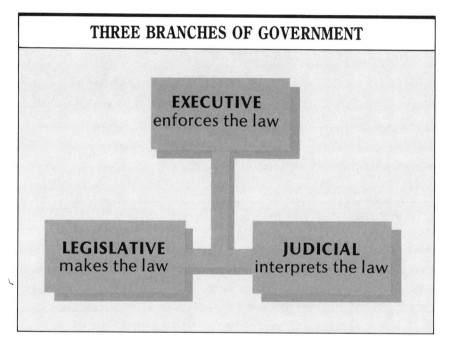

THREE BRANCHES OF GOVERNMENT

EXECUTIVE
enforces the law

LEGISLATIVE
makes the law

JUDICIAL
interprets the law

Executive Branch

The governor heads the executive branch of government in the state. The governor is chosen by the voters.

To be a governor a person must be at least 30 years of age. He or she must also have been a citizen of the state ten years before the election. In Maryland the governor may serve only two terms. Each term is four years long. Here are some of the governor's jobs:

- See that the laws are obeyed.
- Prepare a budget for using the state's money.
- Make many speeches and visit many groups to explain his or her ideas and plans.

William Donald Schaefer became governor in January 1987. He is a member of the Democratic party.

• Help his or her party make a good plan for the state.
• Work with the representatives to get bills passed.
• Sign bills into law or *veto* (kill) them.

WHO DOES THE JOB?

ACTIVITY

The governor doesn't do all the work of the executive branch alone. There are many *departments* with workers. Each department has someone at its head. These department heads answer directly to the governor. Here is a list of some of them. See if you can match the title with the job each does.

1. Collects taxes
2. Heads the state law office
3. Keeps records of the state's money
4. Heads the executive branch

a. Secretary of the Treasury
b. Governor
c. Comptroller
d. Attorney General

Answers: 1. c., 2. d., 3. 1., 4. b.

Legislative Branch

The legislative branch of government makes the laws. We call our Maryland *legislature* the General Assembly. Like our

This is where the state Senate meets. Why do you think some of the chairs on the Senate floor are empty?

United States legislature, the Maryland General Assembly has two parts, or houses. The "upper house" is known as the Senate. The "lower house" is called the House of Delegates. The General Assembly meets in the State House in Annapolis each year for 90 days. The meeting begins on the second Wednesday in January. It can last longer than 90 days, but that is very unusual. People may go to the State House and watch the meetings.

The officer in charge of the Senate is called the President of the Senate. The leader of the House of Delegates is called the Speaker. Both houses elect their own officers. They set rules for carrying out their own business.

The state is divided into 47 voting districts. The voters in each district elect 1 senator and 3 delegates. Altogether there are 47 senators and 141 delegates in the state. The members of both houses are elected at the same time as the governor, every four years.

TO BE A MEMBER OF THE HOUSE OF DELEGATES A PERSON MUST:

1. be a citizen of the United States.

2. be at least 21 years old.

3. have lived in Maryland for three years before becoming a candidate.

TO BE A MEMBER OF THE SENATE A PERSON MUST:

1. be a citizen of the United States.

2. be at least 25 years old.

3. have lived in Maryland for three years before becoming a candidate.

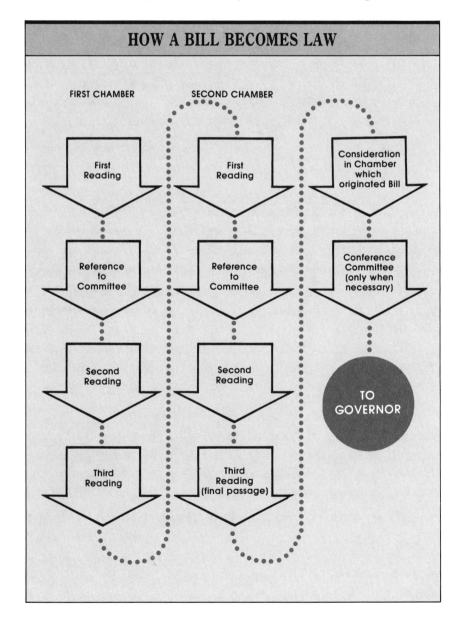

HOW A BILL BECOMES LAW

FIRST CHAMBER

SECOND CHAMBER

First Reading

First Reading

Consideration in Chamber which originated Bill

Reference to Committee

Reference to Committee

Conference Committee (only when necessary)

Second Reading

Second Reading

Third Reading

Third Reading (final passage)

TO GOVERNOR

WHO IS YOUR REPRESENTATIVE?

Find out who represents you in the General Assembly. What are the names of your delegates and senator? Do you know where they live? Do you know how to reach them in their offices? What subjects are important to them? What other jobs do they have when they are not working in Annapolis?

ACTIVITY

How a Bill Becomes Law

A written idea for a law is called a *bill*. A bill can be entered in either house by its *sponsor*. The sponsor is a member of the legislature. The bill is "put into the hopper" and given a number. It is pulled out sometime later.

The bill is then read aloud to the whole group and assigned to a committee. The committee members study how the bill would affect people. Interested people may come to the committee to speak for or against the bill. Then the committee may suggest changes. Sometimes they don't do anything at all with a bill. In this way many bills die in committee. The committee has a great deal of power in deciding which bills will become laws. If the bill passes the committee, it goes back to the whole house. After some debate, the members there may pass it or vote against it. When more than half of the members vote for the bill, it is sent to the other house. There it goes through the same process.

If the bill passes both houses it is sent to the governor. The governor can sign or veto the bill. When the governor signs a bill, it becomes a law. If the bill is vetoed, it goes back to the two houses. If both houses pass it by a $3/5$ majority, or 60%, it becomes law. In this way the General Assembly may override the governor's veto.

Judicial Branch

The judicial branch of government is made up of the courts. They settle all matters involving the laws. Maryland has four levels of courts. Each one handles certain kinds of cases.

Inside a courtroom, the judge sits behind his desk. Lawyers must ask permission to approach the "bench" to speak to the judge.

DISTRICT COURT	Traffic violations and lesser crimes
CIRCUIT COURT	Divorces, adoptions, land titles, and major crimes
SPECIAL APPEALS COURT	Reviews decisions of circuit court
COURT OF APPEALS	Reviews cases from the circuit court; has the final say on the death penalty

If a person feels he or she did not receive a fair trial in one court, their case may be taken to the next highest court. This is called an *appeal*. The highest court in the state is the Maryland Court of Appeals.

WHERE WOULD THE CASE BE HEARD?

ACTIVITY

Divide into groups. Decide in which court the following cases would be heard. The group with the most right answers wins.

1. Ms. X is charged with bank robbery.

2. Mr. Y is found guilty of murder and sentenced to death.

3. Betsy's foster parents want to adopt her.

4. Mr. and Mrs. Z want a divorce.

5. A group of teenagers are accused of disturbing the peace.

6. One person wishes to sue another person for breach of contract in a business deal.

Local Government

There are two kinds of local government: county and *municipal*. These governments are closer to the people than state and federal governments are. For this reason, they are able to take care of a neighborhood's, town's, or city's needs more quickly.

These governments have the power to collect taxes. The taxes pay for the police and fire departments. They also pay for the building and repairing of roads. Many other services, like trash removal, are paid for with tax money.

Repairing pot holes in the road is part of the work of the city street department.

The city of Salisbury runs a zoo. Here workers are preparing the different meals for some of the zoo animals.

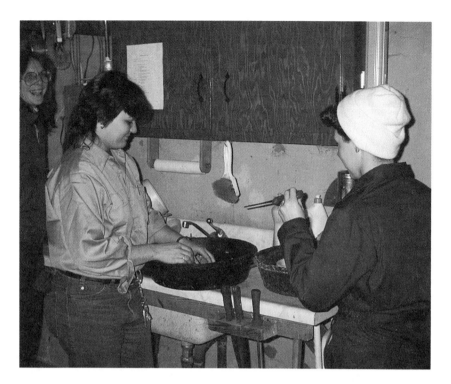

Bringing fresh water to citizens is one service of municipal governments. These men work at the water treatment plant in Salisbury.

Salisbury has a fire unit that operates from the water. This is necessary to protect buildings along the waterfront. The Salisbury fire boat can pump 2,000 gallons of water a minute.

The county carries out some programs for the state and the federal governments. Food stamps and health clinics are some of these programs. Each county must have a public school system.

Municipal governments provide police and fire protection. They usually take care of seeing that a town has a clean water supply. They take care of street lighting and snow plowing in winter. Can you think of other things your municipal government does for its citizens? You might ask some adults to help you make a list.

FINDING COUNTY SERVICES

In the telephone directory find the listing for your county government. Read the list of offices your county has. Figure out what each office would do for the people.

ACTIVITY

Divide into teams. Each team selects a county office or agency. With the help of a grownup, write down many things this department would do for the public. Then write on cards questions that you could ask the other groups about your agency. Be sure to put the answers on the backs of the cards.

Each team asks their questions to the other teams. Correct answers are each worth one point. The team with the most points wins.

Summary

We have learned about governments at four levels: federal, state, county, and municipal. At each level, the work of government is divided among three branches: legislative, executive, and judicial. Citizens pay taxes so governments are able to provide different kinds of services.

Citizens have responsibilities to help government run smoothly. Voting is one way. Being an informed citizen is another way. Even though you are young, you have responsibilities to obey laws. Your government representatives welcome your ideas. There are many ways you can take part in government. Doing so will help prepare you for the time when you will be a voter.

STUDY

WORDS TO KNOW

appeal	nominate
bill	primary
candidate	register
department	representative democracy
general election	sponsor
Independent	third party
legislature	veto
municipal	

QUESTIONS TO ANSWER

1. What is government?
2. Name the four levels of government we live under.
3. What is the person that a party selects to run for office called?
4. What kind of government does our country have?
5. What are four things a citizen can do to help representative government work well?
6. What is a constitution?
7. What is the separation of powers?
8. Who heads the executive branch of government in our state?
9. What are the two parts of the General Assembly?
10. If the governor vetoes a bill, what percent of each house must pass it again for it to become law?
11. Name the four different courts in Maryland.
12. What are the two kinds of local government?

INTERPRETING WHAT YOU HAVE READ

13. To whom would you write to share your idea for a new state song?
14. When a community grows large enough to need a new school, who takes care of that need?
15. It is November 7 and you have just moved to Maryland from Pennsylvania within the past forty days. Your cousin is running for governor. Can you vote for him?

THINGS TO DISCUSS

16. Which level of government provides the services most needed by your family?
17. Does municipal government have a better chance to meet the needs of the people than does state government? Explain your answer.

View of the Chesapeake Bay, with Thomas Point Lighthouse. Keeping the water clean enough for fish and humans takes planning and work.

Maryland Today

17

Maryland is Different Today

The state of Maryland is very different from the colony started in 1634. The colonists were *isolated* in the New World. Their main goal was surviving in their new *environment*. Today, protecting this environment is a major goal.

Ecology of the Chesapeake Bay

In 1984 Governor Harry Hughes began a campaign named "Save the Bay." Money was set aside for research and to uphold the laws that had already been made to protect the bay. Maryland asked Pennsylvania and Virginia to join in cleaning up the Chesapeake Bay. The governors of all three states met and promised to work together on the problem of pollution.

Conservation groups have been working for years to inform the public about pollution. People in these citizens' groups also attend committee meetings of the General Assembly. They want better and stronger laws to protect the Chesapeake Bay.

More than four million people live in Maryland. Most of them get their water from the tributaries of the Chesapeake

Bay. These waters are not clean. The people who get their water from wells also have trouble with pollution.

Chemical Pollution

Chemicals that are used to kill animal and plant pests often cause problems to the ecology. Now there are strict laws limiting their use.

Some wild animals have become rare because of the chemical pollution. The osprey and the bald eagle are two such animals. Because more wildlife *refuges* have been set aside, both of these animals are growing in numbers.

Nitrogen and phosphorous in reasonable amounts are helpful to plants in the bay. If too much of these chemicals is in the water, *algae* grows in huge amounts. The algae blocks out the sunlight for the plants below it. As it decays it uses up the oxygen needed by the animals.

Ospreys once were on the endangered list. Now their numbers are growing. Ospreys eat fish. They dive into the water and grab the fish with their talons.

Some of the nitrogen and phosphorous comes from sewage treatment plants. Nitrogen and phosphorous are also found in fertilizer. It washes from the fields and lawns into the streams. Many businesses also use harmful chemicals. It is now the law that soap cannot contain these chemicals.

Erosion and Sediment Problems

Erosion is the wearing away of the soil. This wearing away is caused by tides, currents, and storms. The many boats that cause waves add to the problem. Some erosion is expected, however, and cannot be stopped.

Land that is plowed or loosened will erode into the streams in larger amounts than if it is covered with grass and trees. *Sediment* is the material that enters the water and sinks to the bottom. Much of the soil that erodes settles in the small streams, but some of it is carried to the bay.

As sediment is dropped near the mouths of rivers, marshes are formed. These areas can then be filled in more easily by developers, who build houses on them. Then the wildlife is sometimes unable to find new places to live.

The sediment that settles in the bottom of the bay smothers plants and animals that live there. Sediment floating

This photograph shows the sediment problem along the Sassafras River. Dirt washes from farm land into the river and begins to fill up the river channel. What different things might happen to the river if too much sediment comes in?

in the water blocks the sunlight needed by the plants.

Erosion has changed the shoreline. For example, Sharp's Island has disappeared completely. Three hundred years ago it was a 600-acre plantation. The place of William Claiborne's settlement is also believed to be under water now. Point Lookout once held a Civil War hospital and prison. The remains of many of these buildings are now under water.

New laws are being written to help solve problems of erosion and sediment. Farmers are helping by planting their rows in patterns that are less likely to erode.

Toxic Waste

Toxic waste in the tributaries of the Chesapeake Bay has received much attention lately. Many kinds of waste change when they enter the water. It is harder to get rid of harmful

By cultivating the rows in different patterns, farmers can help keep soil in the fields and out of nearby rivers. This corn field in Kennedyville is part of a contour strip farm.

wastes that do not change. These are called toxic wastes. Some of these wastes are gasoline, oil, and metals.

Toxic wastes enter the bay in many different ways. Some come from factory waste. The lead from gasoline motors goes into the air and comes down when it rains. Boats sometimes leak gas and oil. Paint used for ships contains copper.

It takes millions of dollars to pay for the testing needed to get rid of factory waste in harmless ways. Businesses find it very costly to get rid of their waste without hurting the ecology.

Problems of the Watermen

The watermen are people who harvest fish and shellfish from the bay and rivers. They are seeing fewer oysters, clams, and fish each year. Some kinds of fish have disappeared completely from some parts of the bay.

The fish that *spawn* in fresh water have been hurt the worst. It is already against the law to catch striped bass, or rockfish, in Maryland. Young rockfish are being raised in hatcheries and later moved to the bay. It is hoped that cleaning up the water and not catching them will allow their numbers to grow.

There are not as many oysters as there once were. The

Mike Fazenbaker is an employee at the Joseph Manning Hatchery in Cedarville Forest. He is netting some striped bass that will be planted in a river.

Watermen use large tongs to gather oysters.

watermen make their money harvesting oysters during the winter months. Now there is less and less oystering. In 1880 there were about 120 million pounds of oysters shucked. In 1980 there were only about 20 million pounds of oysters shucked. Crabs seem to have survived the pollution of the bay better than most other sealife.

There are fewer fish near the western shore of the bay. This is where population and industry have increased the most.

Business and Community Problems

Cities and towns are having to put in costly sewage and water treatment plants. Building construction had to stop in some counties until they got larger sewer systems. This meant fewer jobs in their counties for a time.

Some farmers have to leave a grassy strip around their fields to prevent erosion and fertilizer runoff. This means there is less land to farm. The farmers grow smaller crops and make less money.

A factory might decide it cannot afford to change its waste system and close down. Factory workers would lose their jobs. How would other people get the factory's product? How will the people who are out of work earn a living?

America in Miniature

Maryland is like a small mirror reflecting the United States. It has different kinds of land, water, and climate. Changes that take place in Maryland are like the changes in the rest of the United States. There is less farming now than before. There are more scientific, technical, and aerospace industries. Leisure time and tourism are growing. Historic events and places are getting more attention and care. Maryland's nickname, "America in Miniature," suits the state well. Let's learn how our state is different from place to place.

Southern Maryland

The counties in southern Maryland are St. Mary's and Calvert. The waterfront is still important to each of these counties. It is no longer used for shipping tobacco. The waterfront is now mainly used for recreation. Coves and inlets have hundreds of pleasure boats. Some of the boats are lifted from the water by big fork lifts and stacked on shelves when not in use. There are more boats registered in Maryland than there are cars. Seafood restaurants are part of the many waterfront communities. Southern Maryland is a favorite vacation spot.

Most of Saint Mary's County is rural. Lexington Park is

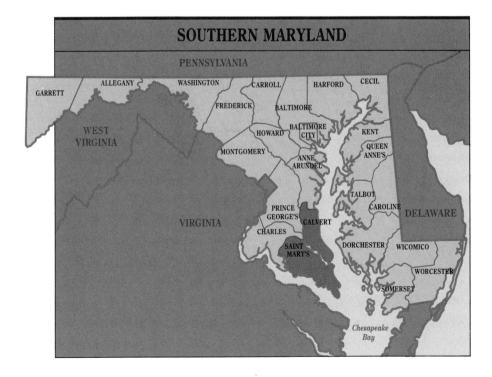

its largest city. The Patuxent Naval Air Station is there. The site of the first settlement, Saint Mary's City, is being restored by the state.

Some people in Calvert County have tried to keep it rural. Still, its population doubled from the 1960s to the 1980s. The area close to Prince Frederick has the largest number of people.

In southern Maryland the main crops are corn, soybeans, and tobacco.

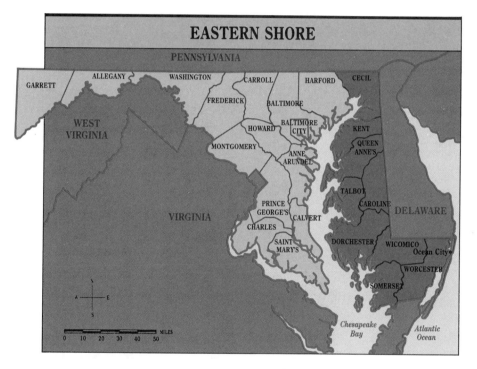

Eastern Shore

The Eastern Shore is divided into nine counties: Cecil, Kent, Queen Anne's, Talbot, Caroline, Dorchester, Wicomico, Somerset, and Worcester. This part of the state changed very little for many years. Now it raises the state's most valuable farm product, broiler chickens. It also has a resort, Ocean City. The Eastern Shore's seafood harvest is threatened by pollution.

OCEAN CITY

I ndians were the first people to recognize the beauty of the island now called Ocean City. When the white people came to this area the Indians left.

Ocean City used to be called Arcadia. There are many stories about pirates who buried treasure there. Much time and money have been spent looking for these treasures. Little is known about any treasure being found.

Until 1916 most people traveled to Ocean City by train. A new highway bridge was then built to the island as more cars were used. Part of the famous boardwalk was laid during the 1880s. Today it covers three miles.

After World War II more and more building took place. More families wanted to spend their vacations near the ocean. Property became very valuable. When the ferry between the western and eastern shores was replaced by the Bay Bridge, even more vacationers began to visit.

By 1965 whole blocks of pastel-colored cottages vanished. They were replaced by high-rise condominiums. Some are 22 stories high. Even before they are finished the buildings are sold out. The result is a great change in the Ocean City population between the winter and summer months. The number of people who live there year round is about 5,000. There may be 300,000 people in Ocean City on any given summer weekend. The sleepy fishing village has become a major seaside resort.

There are still many acres of farm land on the Eastern Shore. Grain and soybeans have become major crops. Some of the grain is used for chicken feed.

Many rivers and creeks make the Eastern Shore ideal for

A flock of geese lives on and around this pond in Chestertown.

waterfowl and wildlife. Cornfields attract ducks, geese, and swans each fall on their way south. Some remain there for the winter. Thousands of birds stop at the Blackwater Wildlife Refuge near Cambridge. Hunters and bird watchers go to the marshes in search of birds.

Many farms are being sold for housing developments and golf courses. Old houses are being changed to bed and breakfast inns. Marinas and boat yards are everywhere.

Cecil County borders both Pennsylvania and Delaware. Many people drive to these neighboring states on the superhighways to work.

Suburban Maryland

Suburban Maryland includes eight counties: Montgomery, Howard, Carroll, Baltimore, Harford, Anne Arundel, Prince George's, and Charles. This is the state's largest population area. Many industries and high technology businesses are found here. A good number of the people in these counties work in Annapolis, Baltimore, Washington, and cities of northern Virginia. Highways to these cities are crowded each day with bumper-to-bumper traffic.

Historic Annapolis, Inc., played a large part in making downtown Annapolis the place it is today. This group bought old buildings and restored them. It worked to get laws passed to control the kinds of buildings allowed in the downtown area.

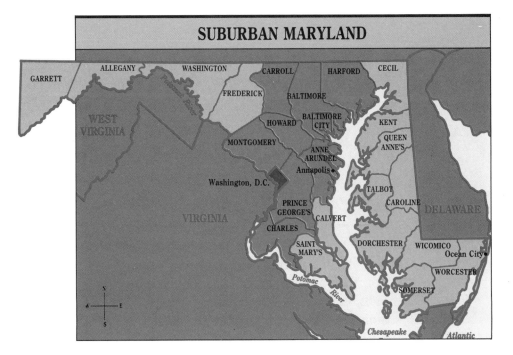

Annapolis is a good example of a city preserving its history and growing, too.

The counties close to Washington, Annapolis, and Baltimore have *dense* populations. Prince George's, Montgomery, and Anne Arundel counties still have some farms.

From the 1950s on, people moved from the older neighborhoods near the cities to the newer suburbs. This caused many changes. Small businesses in the cities lost customers and had to close. People now shopped at the newer suburban malls and shopping centers.

Senior citizens often remained in the older neighborhoods, but they could not get to the malls for shopping. Many of them did not have cars. The Metro rail system running to these communities from downtown Washington has been a help. Now more people are moving to be near the Metro line because it makes getting around easy. Older homes are being fixed up and sold for high prices. Older apartment buildings are being changed to condominiums.

More black, Asian, and Hispanic families are moving to

these neighborhoods close to the cities. Ethnic food stores are to be found in most shopping centers. There are more Indian, Korean, and Mexican restaurants near Washington. Schools that once had many empty classrooms are now filling up again.

Baltimore City, Urban Center

The port of Baltimore is still the greatest business center in Maryland. More people work there than in any other industry in the state. Lately the population of Baltimore City has grown smaller. The population of the counties around it are larger. Many families moved to the suburbs so they could have more room.

Mayor Donald Shaefer led Baltimore City in many restoration projects. People took greater pride in their neighborhoods. Some older buildings that couldn't be repaired were torn down. Many old houses were restored. Old warehouses and factories were changed into apartment buildings.

Downtown Baltimore is growing skyward. Many skyscrapers have been built. The National Aquarium, the Constellation, the Science Center, and the Inner Harbor Pavilions attract thousands of visitors. Baltimore is also a center for the *arts*. It has many concerts, plays, and ballets during the year.

Baltimore still leads the southern ports in the United States in handling standard container freight. It is second on the east coast of the United States and fifteenth in the world.

Classrooms in downtown schools are filling up again since old neighborhoods have been renovated.

Highways and railroads from Baltimore make a good transportation system to the Midwest. Goods can be hauled there from Baltimore faster and cheaper than from other ports in the country. This is known as the *inland advantage*.

Western Maryland

Frederick, Washington, Allegany, and Garrett counties are in western Maryland. Frederick County is rapidly becoming an urban and suburban center. Washington County has been the crossroads for major highways for a long time. Washington County is a rural area, but its people are not far from the city and its services.

Allegany County's coal mines once gave jobs to many

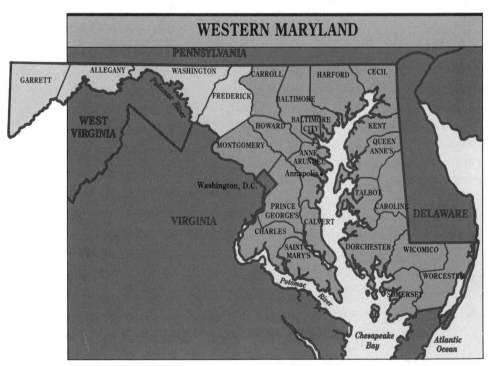

workers. These mines are now closed. Fewer young families are staying in this area because there are not as many jobs. The coal that remains is not very deep in the ground. *Strip mining* is used to remove the coal. Even following government rules, strip mining causes some problems to the water supply.

Strip mining is one way of getting coal and other minerals from the ground. Mining companies often take responsibility for filling in the huge hole and replanting the spot when they have finished.

Acid runoff from the strip mines pollutes wells, springs, and streams.

Some people in the county feel that strip mining should continue because it means jobs. Others feel it should stop because of the pollution.

Garrett County has a few industries, but it is mainly a county of farms and recreation areas. Deep Creek Lake and ski areas attract many tourists.

There are many small industries in these four counties of western Maryland. Craft shops and *factory outlets* dot the highways. Orchards and farms also make money for this area of the state.

Western Maryland has remained a frontier in many ways. It still has forests, wild animals, and beautiful streams. It has fewer people than the other parts of the state. It is less a part of the megalopolis than any other area in the state. Most of the people who live there want it to stay this way.

Looking to the Future

Being close to Washington, D.C., has made Maryland the home of many government workers. Business is good in our state. There are fewer people out of work here than in most other states. Many people move to Maryland each year. The state's future is bright. The "Land of Pleasant Living" will continue to be a pleasant place to live if we all work to make it that way.

Farmers sometimes take their farm produce to town to sell it. This makes it easier for people in the city to buy fresh from the farmer. What is this woman selling from her farm?

STUDY

WORDS TO KNOW

algae
arts
condominium
conservation
dense
environment
factory outlet

inland advantage
isolated
refuge
sediment
spawn
strip mining
toxic

QUESTIONS TO ANSWER

1. From where do most people in Maryland get their water?

2. Name three sources of the chemical pollution in the Chesapeake Bay.

3. What are three causes of erosion?

4. What are the two chief sources of toxic waste in the bay?

5. How have watermen been affected by pollution in the bay?

6. Which two counties are in southern Maryland? What geographic feature is important to them?

7. How many counties make up the Eastern Shore? What most valuable farm product is raised there?

8. How many counties are in suburban Maryland? What action caused many changes in the older areas of these cities?

9. From Baltimore goods can be transported to the Midwest faster than from other ports. What is this called?

10. Is western Maryland an urban or rural area? What kind of mining once provided many jobs but now gives fewer?

11. In what ways is western Maryland like a frontier?

12. Why is Maryland the home of many government workers?

INTERPRETING WHAT YOU HAVE READ

13. How is toxic waste different from chemical pollution?

14. What are some important concerns in our state today?

THINGS TO DISCUSS

15. Suppose you are a farmer and are unable to cultivate your land near the creek that borders your land. Think of ways that this land could be used to make money for you.

16. If a paint factory in Baltimore closed because it could not get rid of its toxic waste, how might the following groups be affected? a) Other paint factories, b) employees, c) shopping malls, d) grocery stores, e) car dealers, f) paint and hardware stores, g) can manufacturers, h) label printers, i) unemployment and welfare departments, j) consumers.

Glossary

abolish (uh-BAHL-ish): put an end to; do away with

abolitionist (a-boh-LISH-un-ust): one who favors doing away with slavery

advantage (ud-VAN-teej): benefit or gain

algae (AL-jee): a large group of lowly plants that cannot be divided into roots, leaves, and stems, and which do not produce seeds

Allies (AL-yz): during World War I, Great Britain, France, and Russia; during World War II, the United States, England, France, and Russia

anti-: opposite or hostile to

architecture (AR-kih-tek-cher): the art of making plans for buildings, or the buildings themselves

Appalachia (ap-uh-LAY-chuh): area of the Appalachian Mountains in western Maryland

appeal: to take action to have a case or decision reviewed by a higher court

arsenal (AR-sun-ul): a place for storing weapons

arts: music, painting, sculpture, dancing, acting, and literature are the arts

assassination (uh-sas-uh-NAY-shun): murdering by secret attack

Assembly: legislative group of the colonists

assembly line: a way of putting something together piece by piece as the thing mechanically passes by the workers

automatic transmission (ah-toh-MA-tik trans-MISH-un): an automobile system of gears that regulates itself

Axis Powers: during World War II, Germany, Italy, and Japan

bale: a bundle of goods such as hay or cotton

Baltimore Clipper: a certain kind of sleek sailing ship

barge: a broad flat-bottomed boat

barter: to trade one thing for another without the use of money

bill: a written idea for a suggested law

Bill of Rights: a part of the state and national constitutions that lists certain rights that each person has

blockade (blahk-AYD): to shut off a place to prevent the coming in or going out of persons or supplies

blockhouse: a strong building with holes in its sides through which a person may shoot out at an enemy

boom town: a town the grows rapidly

bootlegger: a person who makes or sells liquor illegally

boundary (BAOWN-dree): something that marks a dividing line or a beginning or end

bow (BAOW): the forward part of a ship

brackish (BRAK-ish): somewhat salty

campaign (kam-PAYN): a series of activities meant to bring about a certain result

candidate (KAN-dih-dut): one who offers himself or is proposed by others as a suitable person to run for an office

cannery: a factory where food is canned

capital punishment: penalty of death

cargo: goods carried by a ship,

truck, plane, or train

carnivore (KAR-nih-vor): flesh-eating animal

Central Powers: during World War I, Germany, Austria-Hungary, and Turkey

ceremony (SAIR-uh-moh-nee): something done in a regular order as required by law or custom

cesspool (SES-pool): underground catch basin for liquid waste

chandelier (shan-duh-LEER): a branched lighting fixture that usually hangs from the ceiling

charter: an official document granting rights or privileges

chemical warfare (KEM-ih-kul WAR-fair): the use of poisonous and burning gases and chemicals as weapons

climate (KLY-mut): the weather over a long period of time

cockarouse (KAHK-uh-roos): an Indian war captain

colonial (kuh-LOH-nee-ul): having to to do with the thirteen original colonies of the United States

colonist (KAHL-uh-nist): a member of a colony

commercial (kuh-MER-shul): having financial profit as its chief aim

commission (kuh-MISH-un): a group of people given authority to perform certain tasks

communism (KAH-myew-niz-um): a social system in which all things are held in common, usually by the government

complete: having all the needed parts

condominium (kahn-doh-MIN-ee-um): a building divided into units for individual ownership

conservation (kahn-ser-VAY-shun): planned management of natural resources to prevent waste or destruction

constitution (kahn-stih-TOO-shun): the basic principles and laws of a nation

consumption (kun-SUMP-shun): the wasting away of the body, usually by a lung disease

contract (KAHN-trakt): a formal agreement between two or more people

contractor (KAHN-trak-ter): one who oversees the construction of a building

convert: (verb, kon-VERT) to change from one belief or church to another; (noun, KAHN-vert) a person who has changed from one belief or church to another

conveyor belt (kun-VAY-er belt): a wide belt that mechanically carries packages or parts of larger products to be put together

council: an official body of lawmakers or advisors

county seat: a town where a county's government offices are located

craftsman (KRAFTS-mun): a person who is skilled in a trade or handicraft

cultivate (KUL-tih-vait): to prepare land for the raising of crops

customs: taxes charged by governments on imports or exports

cylinder (SIL-un-der): a long round body either solid or hollow

daub and wattle: mud and sticks

debate (dee-BAIT): to discuss a question by giving arguments on both sides

debt (DET): something owed to another

declare: to make known clearly

delegate (DEL-uh-gut): a person sent with power to act for another

dense: thick; packed closely together

department: one of several parts or division of government

depot (DEE-poh): a place where military supplies are kept

depression (dee-PRESH-un): a time of low business activity and widespread unemployment

descendant (dee-SEN-dunt): one who has come down from a certain ancestor or common stock

desert (dee-ZERT): to leave a person or a thing that one should stay with

deserter (dee-ZERT-er): one who leaves a person or a thing he or she should stay with

design (dee-ZYN): to think up or make a pattern or sketch of

developer (dee-VEL-up-er): one who improves land and has buildings built

diagonal (dy-AG-uh-nul): running from one corner to the opposite corner of a four-sided figure

disgracefully (dis-GRAIS-ful-lee): being treated or acting in a way that brings shame

distill: the process of making liquor by letting it fall in drops

draft card: a card that says a young man is able to be called to military service

drainage basin (DRAIN-ij bay-sun): an area of land from which all the runoff water goes into the same river or bay

economic (ek-uh-NAHM-ik): relating to the production, distribution, and consumption of goods and services

economy (ee-KAHN-uh-mee): the way money and goods are used

ecosystem (EE-koh-sis-tum): the way plants and animals interact with their environment

effigy (EF-uh-jee): a crude statue or dummy representing a hated person

elected representative: a person chosen by a group of voters to act for them

elevation (el-uh-VAI-sun): the height of land as measured above or below sea level

employ (em-PLOY): to hire someone to work

environment (en-VY-run-munt): the surroundings in which a person, plant, or animal lives

erode: to wear away by action of water, wind, or sand

erosion (ee-ROH-zhun): the act of wearing away or being worn away

estate (es-TAIT): all of a person's belongings and property left at the time of death

estuary (ES-chew-air-ee): an inlet or arm of the sea, especially the wide mouth of a river

executive (eg-ZEK-yew-tiv): having to do with the branch of government that sees that laws are carried out

export: to send from one country to another; goods sent out of a country

factory outlet: a place in which a certain product is sold at a cheaper price than normal

fall line: a division between the solid rock of the Piedmont and the Coastal Plain deposits

fell: to cut down a tree

ferry: (verb) to carry by boat over water

fertile (FER-tul): capable of growing crops

fiction (FIK-shun): a made-up story

field command: having charge of a large group of people, such as an army group

flax: a plant from which linen is made and which yields livestock feed

flotilla: a group of small ships

fossil (FAH-sul): hardened traces of plant or animal remains

foundation: the base upon which something stands or is grounded

founder: one who establishes a school, company, or town

framework: a basic structure

freemen: in colonial times, men free from slavery or indenture

fringe (FRINJ): a border or trimming

frontier (frun-TEER): the edge of a settled country

galley: the kitchen of a ship

general election: the election in which winners from each party run against each other to determine who will hold office

girdle: a ring made around a tree by stripping its bark

grid: a network of horizontal and perpendicular lines for locating points on a map

gristmill: a place for grinding grain into flour

ha-ha: a sunken kind of fence used in colonial days to keep animals out of the garden

handyman: a man who does odd jobs

harsh: severe or stern

high tech (HY tek): having to do with technology and businesses that work in computers and advanced science

historic district: a place set aside for preserving because its buildings were important in history

hydrographic (HY-droh-GRAF-ik): having to do with the study and mapping of oceans, lakes, and rivers

hymn (HIM): a song of praise especially to God

immigrant (IM-uh-grunt): a person who comes to a country to live

import: to bring into a place or a country

inaccurate (in-AK-yer-ut): faulty, untrue

indentured servant: in colonial times a person who contracted to work for another in exchange for passage to America

independent: not under another's control; belonging to no political party

industry (IN-dus-tree): a branch of business or manufacturing

inherit (in-HAIR-ut): to receive from one's parents or ancestors

inland advantage: being able to transport goods to buyers faster than the competition because of good transportation systems

integration (in-tuh-GRAY-shun): the act of bringing together into common and equal membership, especially bringing together people from different races

interchangeable: capable of being put in each other's place

intersect: to divide by passing through or across

invest: to place money in a business in order to earn a financial return

investor: a person who puts money into a business

irregular: not being perfectly even or smooth

isolated: separated from others

issue (ISH-yew): a matter in dispute

journal (JER-nul): a written account of daily events; a diary

judicial (jew-DISH-ul): relating to the branch of government that is made up of the courts

kerosene (KAIR-uh-seen): thin oil used as a fuel

laborer: one that works at jobs that require strength rather than skill

labor union: an organization of workers formed for the purpose of improving their job situation

landscape architect: a professional whose field of work is decorating and planting gardens and grounds

legal: relating to law

legend (LEH-jund): an old story that is widely accepted as true but cannot be proved so

legislative (LEH-jus-lay-tiv): relating to the branch of government that makes laws

legislature (LEH-jus-lay-cher): a group of people elected to make or pass laws

lock: an enclosure (as a canal) with gates at each end used for raising and lowering boats from one level to the next

loft: an upper room or floor

loot: to rob or steal openly and by force

Loyalist: in colonial times, one who was loyal to England and was against American independence

luxury (LUG-zher-ee): something that adds but is not necessary to one's pleasure or comfort

mainsail: the principal sail on the mainmast of a sailing ship

maneuver (muh-NOO-ver): to guide skillfully

manor: a large estate

manorhouse: the house where the owner of the manor lives

manufacture (man-uh-FAK-cher): the making of products by hand or machinery

manumission (man-yew-MISH-un): being freed from slavery

megalopolis (meg-uh-LAHP-oh-lus): a large, heavily populated area including any number of cities

merchant: one who carries on trade on a large scale

merchant prince: a very rich merchant

metropolis (meh-TROP-oh-lus): a large or important city

midwife: a woman whose work is helping women in childbirth

militia (muh-LIH-shuh): a body of citizens with some military training but called on only in emergency

mortar and pestle: a small, deep bowl with a blunt pounding instrument; herbs and grains may be ground using these tools

municipal (myew-NIH-sih-pul): having to do with the government of a town or city

mussel: a sea animal like a clam having a dark shell and used as food

national anthem: a song of praise honoring the country

natural (NA-cher-ul): made by nature, not humans

navigate (NA-vuh-gait): to travel by water; to steer or direct the course of (as a boat)

necessity (nuh-SES-ih-tee): something badly needed

negotiation (neh-go-shee-AY-shun): the act or process of discussing something for the purpose of reaching a settlement

neutral (NOO-trul): not favoring either side in a quarrel

nominate: (NAH-mih-nait): to name or select to run for office

oath: appeal to God to witness to the truth of what one says

official (oh-FISH-ul): (adj.) approved or authorized; (noun) one who holds an office

omnivore (AHM-nih-vor): a person or animal that eats both animal and vegetable

orator (OR-uh-ter): one who is noted for skill and power in speaking

ornament: something that adorns or adds beauty

outbuilding: a building separate from but near to a main house

overseer: one in charge of watching over the work of a group

patriotic: devoted to one's country

peake: a type of prized shell that served as Indian money

peninsula (peh-NIN-suh-luh): a piece of land extending out into a body of water

pier (PEER): a structure built out into the water for use as a landing place or walk

pioneer: an early settler

plantation: a planted estate tended by laborers

planned community: an area that is designed to be complete with homes, schools, shops, churches, and medical facilities

plateau (pla-TOH): a broad flat piece of high land

pollution (poh-LOO-shun): those things that make something dirty that was clean, for example, impurities in water or air

population: the whole number of people who live in a place

port of entry: a harbor, town, or city where a ship can take on or remove passengers or cargo

pottery: articles made from clay that is shaped while moist and dried with heat

prejudice (PREH-jew-dis): a favoring or dislike of one over another without good cause

preserve (pree-ZERV): to can, pickle, or otherwise prepare for later use

primary: first election in which people from each party are selected to run for office

privateer: an armed private ship sent by a government to attack enemy war ships

process (PRAH-ses): to take a series of steps toward a particular result; for example, to change apples into applesauce

professional (pro-FESH-uh-nul): an occupation not in medicine or agriculture that requires special training

profit (PRAH-fit): the amount remaining after all the expenses are subtracted from the amount received

prohibition (pro-huh-BISH-un): an order to stop the making and sale of alcoholic beverages

protest (PRO-test): a demonstration to show objection to something

proxy: power to act for another

ravaged: laid waste; destroyed; ruined

refuge: a shelter or place of safety

regiment (REH-juh-munt): a military unit made up of any number of smaller units

register (REH-jis-ter): to sign up

religious toleration: accepting and allowing all religions

represent (rep-ree-ZENT): to act for or in the place of someone or something

representative democracy: a form of government in which people are chosen to represent a number of voters

research (REE-serch): a study aimed at discovering new knowledge

resign (ree-ZYN): to give up or quit a post

restore: to give back or make something like it was before

riot (RY-ut): public violence or disorder

roanoke: a type of shell used by Indians as money

root cellar: an underground pit used for storing root crops

run the blockade: to outsail or sneak between other ships trying to block a harbor

sapling: a young, slender tree

savage (SAV-eej): a person belonging to a primitive uncivilized society

seal: a raised design stamped or pressed into paper to show that something is official

seasonal: related to or restricted by a certain season

seasoned: made fit by experience

secession (seh-SEH-shun): withdrawal from a party or group of nations or states

sedan chair: a chair carried on poles above the ground by two or more people

sediment: matter from a liquid that settles to the bottom

sewer system: underground system of pipes that disposes of waste matter

share: an equal part of a company

skirmish: a minor fight in war

sleek: smooth and glossy

slum: a thickly populated area of a city marked by miserable living conditions

smelt: to melt ore to separate or refine the metal

social class: rank in society, often determined by the amount of money one has

spawn: to produce eggs

sponsor: one who takes the responsibility for another person or thing

standardbred: any horse of an American breed developed for trotting or pacing, as a harness racer

stern: rear end of a boat

stock: the sum of money invested in a business; a piece of paper which shows owner-ship of part of a business

stockade: a pen or enclosure made of posts or stakes

stockholder: a person owning stock in a given company

stock market: a place where stocks and bonds are regularly bought and sold

strip mining: to remove minerals from the earth by removing the earth's covering or digging huge holes

suburbia (suh-BER-bee-uh): smaller community outside a city

suffragist (SUF-ruh-jist): a person who believes in allowing women the right to vote

supernatural: relating to something seemingly outside the laws of nature

surplus (SER-plus): the amount left over

survey (SER-vay): to measure and record the outline of any part of the earth's surface

surveyor (ser-VAY-er): one who measures and marks off pieces of land

suspicious (suh-SPISH-us): tending to doubt or distrust

sweat lodge: a teepee where Indian men carried on religious ceremonies that involved sweating as a form of purification

sweat shop: a crowded factory where people worked long hours at low wages, usually being hot and lacking fresh air

symbol: something that stands for something else

taxation without representation: paying taxes to a government without being allowed to have a vote in how the money is spent

tayac (TAY-ak): Indian chief over many chiefs

telescope house: a house where a new part added is larger than the part before it

tenement (TEN-uh-munt): a house divided into separate apartments for rent to families and often meeting only

minimum standards of safety and comfort

third party: any political party in the United States other than Democrat or Republican

thoroughbred (THUR-oh-bred): a horse of the best blood bred through a long line of pure stock

tidal current: flowing and ebbing of the waters with the rise and fall of the tide

toll: a fee paid for the privilege of using a road or bridge

tourism (TOOR-izm): tourist travel

toxic: poisonous

transportation: means of travel

treadmill: a mill worked by a person or animals walking an endless belt

treaty (TREE-tee): an agreement made by negotiation between two or more countries

trencher: a wooden platter for serving food

tributary (TRIH-byew-tair-ee): a stream flowing into a larger stream or lake

turnpike: a road on which one must pay money to travel

Underground Railroad: a system of people and buildings which helped slaves escape to freedom

unconstitutional (un-kahn-stih-TOO-shun-ul): not according to the constitution

uprising: a rebellion or refusal to do something

utensil: a tool or vessel used in a kitchen

vermin: small harmful animals that are hard to get rid of

veto (VEE-toh): forbid; prohibit; refusal to sign a bill into law

violence (VY-oh-luns): the use of physical force to harm a person or property

vision quest (VIH-zhun kwest): a ceremony where a young Indian boy goes alone into the wilderness for a time

volley: a discharge of a number of weapons at once

volunteer (vahl-un-TEER): one who offers himself or herself to do a service for free

wampumpeag: shells used by Indians as money

weir: a fence or enclosure built in a stream for catching fish

welfare: benefits paid to people by the government because of poverty or lack of work

wharf: a structure built on the shore for loading and unloading ships

werowance (WAIR-oh-wuns): Indian chief

wigwam: a dwelling place built of an arched framework of poles overlaid with bark, hides, or rushes

wilderness: an uncultivated or uninhabited region

wiso (WEE-soh): member of a peace council

yeoman (YOH-mun): a freeholder

Acknowledgments and Photo Credits

The authors wish to thank the many people who have lended support and cooperation to this project.

Our sincere appreciation goes to Barbara M. Virvan for hours of work and her expertise in reviewing and making changes in various drafts of the manuscript. We also acknowledge her work in gathering illustrations for the book. Her assistance made our work much easier.

Hearty thanks to Dr. Marianne Alexander, Dr. George Callcott, and Dr. Fred Czarra for reading the manuscript and suggesting changes for its improvement.

We appreciate the initial help given by Wayne Hughes and Clifton Osborne in getting us started on this project.

Special thanks goes to Instructional Resources Corporation, 1819 Bay Ridge Avenue, Annapolis 21403, for their cooperation in furnishing numerous illustrations. Many photos from this book, plus several hundred more, are available from this source through *The History of Maryland Slide Collection.* Also available from Instructional Resources Corporation are *The American History Slide Collection* and *The Western Civilization Slide Collection.* For more information you may call collect, 301-263-0025.

Numerous other people and organizations were helpful in obtaining illustrations. We wish to give special acknowledgment to the following: Charles Shoup for his photography services, Kate Anderson, Annapolis Tourism, the Benjamin Banneker Museum of Annapolis, Robert F. Eagen of the Environmental Protection Agency, the personnel of Fort McHenry, Frederick Historical Society, Ada Schrock of Garrett County, Historic Annapolis, Image Finders, Mrs. Alfred Wright of the Kent Island Historic Society, the Lillie Mae Carroll Museum of Balitmore, Al Rosenthal of the Maryland Department of Natural Resources, Catherine A. Wallace of the Maryland-National Capital Park and Planning Commission, Prince George's Historical Society, Chief Henry Darling of the Salisbury Fire Department, Mervin Savoy, Karen Stafford of the St. Mary's Commission, Sotterly Plantation, and Westminster Carol County Farm Museum.

The specific pictures used in this book are credited below. The authors and publisher also wish to thank those who offered pictures that could not be used for lack of space. Letters beside the numbers designate position on the page: T (top), B (bottom), L (left), and R (right).

Chicago Historical Society, 208

Dover Publications, from Thomas Harriot, *A Briefe and True Report of the New Found Land of Virginia, 1972 reprint of 1590 edition,* 29, 31T, 37, 39

Index